BIRMINGHAM

PAST AND PRESENT

THE CITY CENTRE

Volume 2

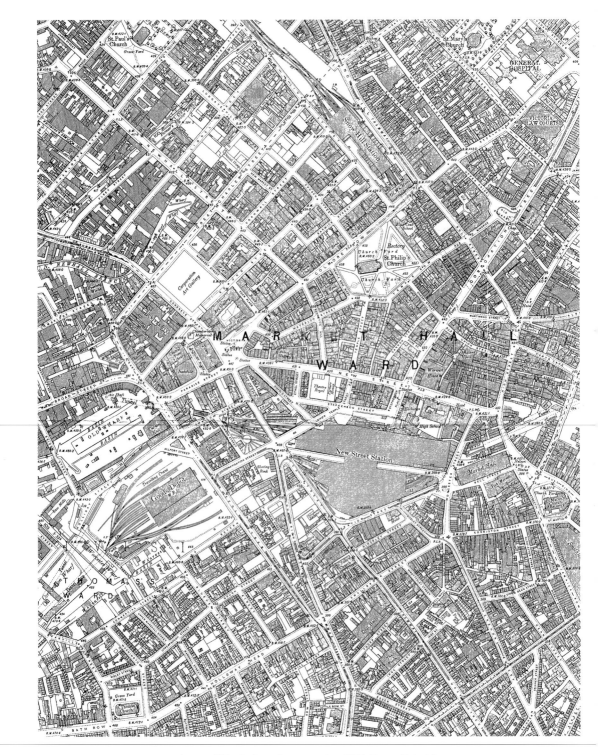

A map of Birmingham city centre circa 1903. *Crown Copyright*

BIRMINGHAM

PAST AND PRESENT

THE CITY CENTRE

Volume 2

DAVID HARVEY M.ED.

·THE HERITAGE OF BRITAIN·
from
The NOSTALGIA Collection

First published in 2003

British Library Cataloguing in Publication Data

A catalogue record for this book is available from the British Library.

ISBN 1 85895 186 0

Past & Present Publishing Ltd
The Trundle
Ringstead Road
Great Addington
Kettering
Northants NN14 4BW

Tel/Fax: 01536 330588
email: sales@nostalgiacollection.com
Website: www.nostalgiacollection.com

Printed and bound in Great Britain

Past and Present

A Past & Present book
from
The **NOSTALGIA** *Collection*

ACKNOWLEDGEMENTS

This book would not have been possible without the many anonymous photographers whose hobby or job it was to capture a scene or an event. Many commercial photographers were employed to show buildings under construction or newly completed, while prestigious redevelopment schemes were comprehensively followed on film from the late 19th century through to the huge present-day schemes in and around the Bullring. It would take too long to thank every photographer individually, but all are acknowledged beneath their photographs. Sincere thanks are due to Malcolm Keeley, who unearthed a number of gems, and to Roger Carpenter, who allowed me access to the Joe Moss and A. W. V. Mace photographic collections. Special thanks, however, are due to the staff of the Local Studies Department of the Birmingham Central Reference Library, and especially to Peter Drake, who allowed me into the 'stacks' normally never seen by the general public, and a free rein to use their huge photographic archive. Stephen Hopkinson of John Whybrow Limited generously allowed me access to their wonderful photographic collection. The picture files held by the City Engineers & Public Works Department were also invaluable and were made readily available. The Birmingham Roman Catholic Archdiocesan Archives were kindly made available through the good services of His Grace The Archbishop of Birmingham.

Thanks are due to Barry Ware for his advice, which is always generously given, to the careful proof-reading of Richard Weaver, and to the patience of my wife Diana, without whose support, proof-reading and grammatical expertise this volume would have not been possible.

CONTENTS

PREFACE

British cities such as Belfast, Glasgow, Liverpool, Manchester and Newcastle, for example, are constantly changing their face for a variety of reasons. Birmingham is another, but perhaps its central area has altered more times than nearly anywhere else. The reasons for these changes are organic and economic, political and entrepreneurial, while historical events such as bomb damage in the Second World War and the changing needs of people living in and commuting into the city have all contributed to the dynamics that are variously called change, folly, growth, carbuncles or imaginative.

At the dawn of the photographic period, in the early years of Queen Victoria's reign, when the first huge, wooden plate cameras were being lugged about, Birmingham, although recently booming from the growth of both its own specialised industries as well as benefiting from the heavy industries of the Black Country, was little more than a fairly large market town. It was just beginning to compete with the other large centres of population in the central Midlands, such as Coventry and Wolverhampton, for the position of main regional centre. Although it had the advantage of being at the hub of the national canal 'silver cross', the fledgling railways were still being developed, although promising links to the capital and other large centres of manufacturing were developing. Yet 30-odd years later, by the mid-1870s, the Birmingham of 'Uncle Joe' Chamberlain was being transformed into a sophisticated shopping centre with a planned street pattern that would be the envy of what had become other thriving regional centres.

This late thriving of the commercial heart of

Birmingham and the Victorian civic pride resulted in the development of the city centre that is still there today, a city centre that again was captured on film by a later generation of local Victorian photographers such as Thomas Lewis, Henry Joseph Whitlock, Benjamin Stone and John Whybrow. The attentions that Birmingham received during the Second World War led to Cadbury publishing a somewhat jingoistically titled book *When We Build Again*, and sure enough, out of the dereliction came the 'promised land' for all up-and-coming urban planners who were wedded to concrete, the speeding motorcar and troglodyte pedestrians. Out-of-date schemes such as the 1930s-designed Inner Ring Road placed a concrete collar around the city, which although ideal for university students of urban geography to identify as the Central Business District (CBD), effectively made the trend- setting Bull Ring Shopping Centre an expensive 'white elephant' on

The market being held in the **BULL RING** in about 1890 had perhaps not much changed in several hundred years. A market had been held in Birmingham since the mid-1150s, when King Henry II gave the small village a Charter to hold such a function every Thursday. Over the succeeding centuries, separate meat, vegetable and fish markets developed in the Jamaica Row and Moat Row areas, as well as the famous Charles Edge-designed Market Hall, opened in 1834. Yet despite all this competition, the open-air Bull Ring market continued to thrive, and its legacy was to be found in the open spaces in front of the old Bull Ring Centre, demolished after a life of only 40 years.

The statue of Admiral Horatio Nelson looks over the canvas-roofed stalls as the lavender-sellers, the two women with the white aprons, sell their sweet-smelling bunches. Flowers, including violets, were popular as they helped to mask the appalling smells coming out of the middens and earth closets that were so common in the inner areas of the town's back-to-back courtyards. All of the men are true to the tradition of the end of the 19th century, wearing either caps, derbies, bowlers and top hats. Almost all the women are wearing black clothing – only the woman on the left is wearing something colourful, in this case a tartan shawl – and walking up the Bull Ring is a man wearing workmen's leggings.

Despite the fact that this fascinating view is more than 110 years old, people are doing just what they do today, looking around the various stalls for either a bargain or something that catches the eye. *J. Whybrow collection*

the wrong side of the Ring Road! Again all the demolition was faithfully recorded on film by Birmingham's City Engineers Department, revealing what a wealth of attractive and historically important buildings were put to the demolisher's ball and chain, and it was only after the end of the 1970s that older buildings, or at least their original frontages, were retained.

Throughout the 1970s and much of the 1980s the city lost its way and its confidence, as one traditional industry after another closed down, but in the late 1980s the City Council 'bit the bullet' and, by realising that the old heavy industries had gone for ever, were able to build a new Birmingham based around conference facilities, the leisure industry, tourism and technology. Suddenly the Inner Ring Road was being lowered or even demolished, people were appearing on the surface of streets once again, and the developments along Broad Street, with the International Convention Centre, Centenary Square and Brindleyplace, being architectural as well as economic 'honeypots', extended the old traditional Central Area westwards to Five Ways. The re-opening of Snow Hill Station as well as the rebuilding of the lovely Edwardian Moor Street Station, undertaken with Chiltern Trains and the developers of the new Bullring, will enliven the transport services to the south of the city, while the extension of the Metro Light Rapid Transit System (a tram!) out of Snow Hill and into the city centre streets to New Street, Victoria Square and Broad Street to terminate at Five Ways will further enhance the city's status as the main regional shopping centre. The photographers of the 21st century will record these changes, the 'before' scenes, the demolition, the construction and the shiny new finished product with all the same enthusiasm as their forebears. For the traditionalists, the 'new' Moor Street Station will allow steam locomotive-hauled trains back into the city centre thanks to the 'Shakespeare Specials' operated to Stratford-upon-Avon by the Birmingham Railway Museum at Tyseley.

The new Bullring (note the new development's revised spelling), approaching completion at the time of writing, is Europe's largest retail regeneration project, with two large department stores, nine major space users, over 100 shop units, and employment for 8,000 people. It is so large that when fully operational it will add around 40 per cent extra shops to the existing city centre, and for the first time since the early 1960s it will bring the Bull Ring and the surrounding regeneration area back into the city centre once again. Further to the east, the Millennium Point 'people-friendly' science, technology and learning area of museums, leisure facilities and Discovery Centre in Digbeth, is being linked to the city by demolishing the elevated Masshouse Circus, which will allow access by way of tree-lined boulevards, as well as the redevelopment of the Birmingham & Fazeley Canal along the same lines as the highly successful Gas Street Basin regeneration, creating a new area of trees and parkland to be known as City Park. This is outside the scope of this book, though with the expansion of the city centre to the south-east, in ten years time a similar Birmingham volume might include a chapter on the East Side development, just as these two *Past and Present* volumes included the 1990s regeneration of the highly successful Broad Street area.

All city centres are organic and Birmingham is no exception; it is constantly changing, and as soon as a chapter in a book, a video or a television programme about it has been finished it will be out of date, as one old landmark is pulled down and replaced by something new and vibrant. And that is how it should be! Dear reader, this is not a book about now, nor the future, but captures the way Birmingham was just seconds ago, when the last photograph was taken, as well as how it has changed over the last 160 years.

Bull Ring, Birmingham   13523

Twenty years after the date of the photograph on page 6 the **BULL RING** is still frequented by lavender and flower sellers, though the young girls' skirts have shortened by this time. W. Fisher, the florist, whose sign is above his stall, seems to be doing very little trade, while in the foreground one of the other stallholders alters his display of flowers. Lord Nelson still stands benevolently over the market place, having no doubt recently listened to one of the many orators who used the statue as a place from which to talk to any passer-by about the politics of the day or some social inequality. In the distance is St Martin's Church standing at the junction of Spiceal Street and the Bull Ring, which apparently has not yet been fitted with the overhead for the 'new-fangled' electric trams. The Holt's public

house was the Lion and Lamb, which stood opposite Phillips Street. It was only one room wide and had been called The Comet. The whole of this block was destroyed by the air-raid on the night of 9 and 10 April 1941.

The 1960s open-air market in front of the Bull Ring Centre stood in the 'hole' that was St Martin's Circus. The problem with the location of the Bull Ring Market was that it was half hidden by the roads that circulated above it, and was inaccessible to pedestrians as it could only be reached by subways. The market area, although more geographically focused than its predecessor, went through many different 'revamping' programmes, but nothing could disguise its increasing shabbiness. Yet the Brummie was still attracted to it, and it has taken more than the

dreaded planners to destroy the traditional heart of the city and to kill off the 'homing instincts' of the good citizens of Birmingham to 'their market'. This is where plastic household kitchenware bargains could be found among the rows and rows of hanging clothes, where fresh fruit and vegetables vied with the exhaust fumes percolating down from the road above, which in turn were masked by the smells emanating from a cheap perfume stall. Yet whatever the Bull Ring had become, it was still a place of vibrancy and interest, even in this reincarnation, despite being in its death throes before its demolition in 2001. The replacement Bull Ring Market, it has to be hoped, will recapture the Brummie's heart once again. *Author's collection/DRH*

BRUMMIES

What is a Brummie? Well, it is more than someone born in the City of Birmingham. It is someone whose flat regional accent has been lampooned, and because of that people have regarded the Brummie as someone who is uneducated and uncultured. How wrong they are! Birmingham folk have a tradition of hard work and industry that stretches back to the 15th century, when visitors to the town remarked on the constant toil and sounds of hammers and forges.

This tradition has carried through from industries with origins in the Industrial Revolution. In the cramped, frequently squalid Dickensian conditions of the 19th century, through sheer hard work Birmingham carved out a reputation of being the 'City of a Thousand and One Trades'. It was said that nowhere in the British Empire did the sun set without glinting on something that had been made in Brummagem. The skilled jewellery trades developed out of the medieval trinket and button trade, with Birmingham getting its own Assay Office in August 1773. Gun-making transferred from the Digbeth area into the Weaman Estate, near what is now Steelhouse Lane, in the late 1720s, while many brassworks developed near Broad Street. A wide range of industries and toolmaking developed throughout the 19th century, and the dour, hard-working Brummie was born, with a dark sense of humour, perhaps keeping ferrets or whippets, and living 'cheek by jowl' with his place of work.

Brummies inherited a dialect that William Shakespeare would have recognised, but in later years the migration of people into the town from Shropshire and Wales, from rural Warwickshire, Worcestershire and Oxfordshire and even further afield, began a tradition that continues today and gives the Brummie a more cosmopolitan air.

As people became more affluent towards the end of the Victorian period, they began to require their own means of transport. Cycle-manufacturing had a certain focus in the West Midlands, and Birmingham quickly became one of the major centres for the new 'Safety' bicycle. From this it was only a small step to the motorcycle industry. More than 100 motorbike makers can claim to have been based in Birmingham over the years, many of which developed into car manufacturers. Long-forgotten builders such as Abingdon, Alldays and Onions, Calthorpe and Lanchester, not to mention Austin, BSA, Rover, Morris-Commercial, Wolseley and Singer, were just some of the city's manufacturers. Virtually all had factories out in the suburbs, well beyond the scope of this book, but all contributed to the reputation of the Birmingham of the 1960s, giving it the epithet of 'Car City'.

In time the word 'Brummagem' came to mean 'cheap' or 'counterfeit', and it took many years to rid the city's products of that reputation. Conversely, by the end of the 19th century Birmingham had a reputation as a leader in civic amenities such as gas street lighting, a fresh water supply and a sewerage system that was the envy of many other places. Back-to-back housing was banned, a municipal fire service was begun and a new Public Health Committee oversaw improvements in medical provision. In 1891 this thriving industrial Victorian town achieved city status, and a reputation as a place of some culture, with a fine Art Gallery and an annual music festival. In 1909 the University of Birmingham was opened on its 'greenfield' site in Edgbaston, and under the tutelage of Joseph Chamberlain, Birmingham was expertly managed. By the last summer of peace in 1914 it had one of the finest shopping streets of all the provincial cities. All this placed it at the economic heart of early-20th-century prosperity.

Yet the Brummie's heart lay in one particular place in the city – the Bull Ring. This was the focus of the Brummie's allegiance, not Villa Park or St Andrews as it is today; everyone knew and recognised it as belonging to and epitomising Birmingham. Perhaps that is why there has been so much resentment since the 1960s when the heart of the Bull Ring was ripped out for redevelopment, which in turn ripped out the soul of many a citizen of the town.

These photographs do not show the Brummie at work or even at play, but caught in a moment of time just going about the city centre as people are doing at the very moment that you are reading this book.

Below In the days before the motor bus, the electric tramcar was the 'Transport for the Masses'. On a normal Saturday in the 1920s, with a football match at Villa Park, football fans, mingling with the shoppers, are waiting in **MARTINEAU STREET** for the next tram to take them to the game. In the foreground they are queuing for the next 6 service tramcar, which will take them to Trinity Road in Birchfield Road, as the one on the left is already full. At the bottom of the street more men – football in the mid-1920s was

a distinctly male-supported sport – board the service 3 tramcar bound for Witton Square, which was the direct service to Villa Park and stopped only a few yards away from the ground. Open-balconied tramcar 140 is not proving too popular as it waits to leave on the 8 route to Alum Rock. The wonderful gas street lamps were strategically placed to illuminate the tram loading stands, though the tram route destination boards were electrically lit, with the wiring apparently coming off the tramcar overhead.

Martineau Street was first cut between High Street and the newly developed Corporation Street in about 1880, as an important part of Joseph Chamberlain's Improvement Scheme. It seems strange that the Martineau Street of the 1920s, which was so full of business, vigour and activity with the football fans at this major city tram terminus, would be closed in 1961. The late-Victorian shops and offices built in the typically solid-looking Italianate-style buildings would be replaced by an unpopular shopping centre that was named Martineau Square, which at the time of writing is being redeveloped. *Birmingham City Transport*

Above right Now this really is the 'Art of Queuing!' Here is another tram terminus – **NAVIGATION STREET** – in another year, but the effect is still the same. The queue for the tramcars stretches around the corner into Hill Street – with more than 200 people waiting patiently on this summer day, the 'Pure Ices' ice-cream seller is probably doing a good trade. Alternatively the queuers could buy a packet of 'fags' from Finlay's tobacconist kiosk. Standing over the scene is the dark brooding Victorian presence of what by this time was the Central Grammar School. The reason for the queue is not a football match – they are waiting to go to the 'Brummies playground' at the Lickey Hills. The citizens of Birmingham could take a fivepenny ride to the terminus of the 70 tram service at Rednal, cross Lickey Road and there they were, in the Worcestershire countryside.

This 1951 view, with the newly introduced zebra crossing road markings augmenting the pre-war Belisha beacons, represents the beginning of the end of an era. Within a year the Birmingham tramcars along Bristol Road to the Lickeys would be scrapped, finally going altogether on Saturday 5 July 1952. This coincided with the gradual relaxation of post-war food and clothes rationing.

Also, the introduction of the BBC's television service in the Birmingham area with the opening of the Sutton Coldfield television transmitter on 17 December 1949 had a profound effect on social habits. By the mid-1950s the availability of new British motorcars after the post-war 'Export or Bust' period meant that people could venture further than a tram ride to the Lickey Hills, so within a few years the hills, given to the city by the Cadbury family, went from a tourist trap to a nature trail. Queues like this would soon be little more than a memory. *Author's collection*

Right It was realised at the City Centre Symposium, held in March 1988, that there was a need to make the city centre a more pleasant place to shop and a more attractive place to work. There was also a need to improve its rather staid reputation for closing down every night at dusk. The Inner Ring Road's bypass status was transferred to the Middle Ring Road, and thus the 25-year-old stranglehold of the Queensway development was at last addressed. Free pedestrian movement came with the removal of subways and street-level landscaping, and the lowering of the road at Paradise Circus was completed on time and opened on 10 October 1989, while John Bright Street was also pedestrianised during that year. The Martineau Square area, which included Union Street, was designated for pedestrianisation as one of the first attempts to give the city centre back to the pedestrians.

UNION STREET has now been pedestrianised for over a decade, and its 'humanising' for the Brummie has involved additional street furniture and, more recently, the proliferation of street kiosks, including this one for scarves and leather goods. They rely on passing trade and impulse buying, and this stall has several people looking at the wares. Passers-by, however, are in the main doing just that! *DRH*

If the 'heart' of Birmingham for the Brummie was the Bull Ring, then the junction of **CORPORATION STREET** and **BULL STREET** was the retail core of the city. Dominating the junction was the impressive seven-storey Portland stone-faced Lewis's department store. This had been opened in this form in 1929 and was to last until it closed its doors on 13 July 1991. On the Lower Bull Street corner was G. A. Dunn & Co, the gentleman's outfitter and hatter, whose shop fronts even today have the same Arts and Crafts Movement windows. This scene was captured on 19 July 1955 from the first-floor window of Montague Burton's tailors shop, and out of the picture on the left in Bull Street is a Dolcis shoe shop. On the right of Bull Street is the entrance to the Minories, guarded by the columns beyond Lewis's sunblinds.

On the extreme right in Corporation Street, having just been passed by the Bedford CA van behind the Ford Consul EOTA car, is a Midland Red D5-type double-decker. Across the road following the Fordson EO4C van, with its spare wheel mounted on the nearside door, is a Scammell Scarab owned by British Railways. These three-wheeled successors to the 'Mechanical Horse' could be found in almost every town and city in the country that had a railway station; indeed, BR eventually owned more than 7,500 of these most useful tractor units. All but one of the cars parked outside Lewis's in Corporation Street

are British-built: among this cross-section of the British post-war motorcar industry are a late-1930s Ford Tudor 7Y model, a Morris Oxford, a Triumph Mayflower, a Morris Minor Traveller and a couple of Austin A40s, the one at the front being a four-door Devon while the one in front of the Rover 75 is a two-door Dorset.

If there was a spot in Birmingham's infamous one-way-street system, introduced in 1933, that was guaranteed to cause confusion, it was here. All the roads meeting outside Lewis's were one-way, the two halves of Bull Street outbound and the two halves of Corporation Street inbound towards the junction. This junction was 'controlled' by traffic lights for both vehicles and pedestrians, being one of the first places in Birmingham with pedestrian lights. If anyone has ever wondered about the purpose of those little square studs set in the roadway at traffic lights or pedestrian crossings, here is the answer; if a pedestrian was knocked down by a car between the studs they could legitimately claim on the insurance, otherwise they would be considered to have been jay-walking. On this July day there is only a vague 'following of the studs' by the pedestrians, and there are more than 20 people either walking across the strangely shaped traffic island or just meandering across the road. For years, crossing the city-centre streets against the lights was a sport enjoyed by Brummies. *Birmingham Public Works Department*

At the edge of the city centre were Victorian houses that survived until the beginning of the 1970s, and this was the sort of housing in which many Brummies had to live. **GOSTA GREEN** was in medieval times an open common covered with grass and gorse, but by 1967 the grass and gorse had long since disappeared. In the early 1970s these houses had also disappeared, and today the site of this once exrensive 19th-century housing area is buried under the campus of the University of Aston. Artisans' houses were built on the land near Aston Street and Gem Street after the 1860s, although the area had been dominated from about 1840 by T. Rickman's Gothic-styled Bishop Ryder Memorial Church. These two-storey, two-up, two-down properties, with their bricked rear courtyards, were typical of houses that post-dated the 1870 Housing Act. The washing was hung out across the courtyard, which was illuminated at night by the single gas lamp. There are no fewer than 12 galvanised dustbins in the yard, while many of the small rear extensions to the premises are outside lavatories that would have post-dated the houses; when they were built there would have been communal lavatories at one end of the yard. The life-blood of the Brummie was industry, and never far away was the factory. Here in Lawrence Street, as was typical around Birmingham, the factory chimney was just over the wall at the end of the courtyard. Finally, did the footballer who managed to kick the ball lodged on the roof on the left – can you spot it? – ever manage to play for the Villa or the Blues? *Author's collection*

COMMERCE

What constitutes commerce but does not entail retailing can be somewhat difficult to define, but in Birmingham commerce represents any business activity to do with accountancy, banking and the stock exchange, and the legal profession, which usually involves financial dealings. The development of manufacturing and trading in the town left many former merchants in the role of manufacturers, and as such they had the power to set up their own 'money houses' in the late 17th century, establishing the banking profession in the early years of the Hanoverian succession. Birmingham had long been a centre of capital, providing money for local businessmen as well as casting a wider net into the outlying Black Country, which was beginning to develop the coal mines, ironworks and glassworks that would provide the West Midlands with its raw materials and semi-finished products.

A typical example, and one of the more successful, was the industrialist John Taylor, a button-maker, who set up a banking business with the iron-slitting-mill-owner Sampson Lloyd II. The Taylors & Lloyds Bank began trading in 1765 at premises in Dale End, and soon the two families became some of the more dominant financial dealers in the town. This was later to become Lloyds Bank when the Taylors left the company exactly 100 years after its formation. Gradually the former market area around Dale End in the vicinity of Welch Gate changed from this early locational economic function as more central and prestigious buildings gradually replaced what were, in many cases, 18th-century merchants' houses converted into commercial use.

The locating of the commercial heartland of Birmingham stretches back to events not based on commerce itself, but on the selling of land belonging to the Colmore and Newhall estates to the north of the town. The building of St Philip's Church as the new church for the town's gentry was the catalyst for the urban development of this part of Birmingham, but the great impetus came in 1746 when the Colmores began to lay out building plots on a grid pattern. The elegant tree-lined avenue from New Hall, their Jacobean house demolished in 1787, became Newhall Street and led up to Colmore Row on the top of the ridge next to the newly built St Philip's Church. An Act of Parliament allowed the widow of Charles Colmore, the redoubtable Ann Colmore, to dispose of the land on 120-year leases. These long leases were an attempt to retain some control over the construction standards of the new town houses, and had the effect of avoiding the rapid sub-standard housing growth of the mid-19th century that afflicted other parts of the town. Edmund Street was built by 1750, and the land leading down to today's only surviving 18th-century square around St Paul's Church had been built upon by the mid-1780s.

The careful planning of this area to the north of Colmore Row meant that by the time the leases came up for renewal in the 1860s, the numerous banking houses that were scattered across the town (there were only six in 1820) began to see that the impending redevelopment of the area afforded them the opportunity to build new premises on the site of the once majestic but now run-down Georgian town houses. From about 1866 work began on remodelling Colmore Row, and in 1873 the new Barclays Bank building was opened on the corner of Temple Street. Lloyds Bank had been built as early as 1864, to the design of Chatwin, while the Staffordshire Bank in Temple Row behind St Philip's Church was ready in 1887. Around the corner in Waterloo Street the National Provincial Bank had earlier opened new premises in 1833, only three years after the Birmingham & Midland, which became the Midland Bank in 1836, opened its new premises on the corner of Bennetts Hill.

By 1875 J. A. Chatwin's Grand Hotel had been completed in Colmore Row, and suddenly the old Georgian street, which had been so carefully planned, had been transformed within 20 years into a financial and commercial centre for the town. Church Street, opposite St Philip's, continued the area's regeneration with some attractive Arts and Crafts buildings by Newton &

Cheatle in 1898, being outstanding examples of this period of growth. Today the Colmore Row area, bounded by Great Charles Street Queensway to the north and the Town Hall end of New Street to the south, is established as the commercial heartland of the city, accommodating the majority of the city's accountants and solicitors. More recently, it is also where Birmingham's own Stock Exchange has been located.

Elsewhere in central Birmingham, on the corner of Stephenson Place on land owned by the old New Street-sited King Edward VI School, the Birmingham Exchange was built. This was opened in 1865, having been designed by Edward Holmes in a heavily Gothic style. The building contained the Exchange Hall, which was Birmingham's equivalent to the London Stock Exchange, as well as shops, offices and a restaurant. By the start of the 1880s this building had become the site of the offices of Birmingham's first telephone exchange. This lovely piece of Victorian 'rhubarb' was wantonly demolished in the early 1960s as part of the redevelopment of New Street Station, and was replaced by yet another of the many concrete blocks that were considered at the time to be at the 'cutting edge' of city centre redevelopment, but which 40 years later look unattractive and time-expired.

On the other side of Stephenson Place was the delightful, classically designed Midland Bank of 1869, with its coupled marble Ionic columns, which, unlike the long-demolished Exchange Building, has survived as Birmingham's premier Waterstones bookshop. The opening of the Bank of England's Birmingham branch in 1827 meant that safe gold reserves were being circulated as paper money, which could be guaranteed as the 'national currency', making local businesses far more secure. By the time that Spooner & Attwood's Bank closed its doors in 1856, all the town's private banking houses had either disappeared or become part of much larger organisations, leaving just seven joint stock banks to thrive in the business community of Birmingham.

The junction around New Street, Stephenson Place and Corporation Street remained an island in Birmingham's commercial landscape until the 1980s, when commercial pressures caused by the high cost of this premier-site land brought about a move away from this highly desirable junction, except for the Midland Bank (later HSBC). Despite the construction of Brindleyplace, along Broad Street, the majority of the area around Colmore Row has remained the domain of the city's financial dealers, their original Victorian facades often masking entirely new buildings.

The road that was built from Suffolk Street towards the then town centre of Birmingham in the late 18th century was in many ways unique. Although it did originally have housing on the Suffolk Street corner, NAVIGATION STREET was neither a commercial nor a shopping street, but rather a routeway that led into the centre of Birmingham. The construction of New Street Station in a natural amphitheatre, officially opened on 1 June 1854 and originally to be known as Birmingham Central, necessitated the removal of many old houses. It also resulted in much of the town end of Navigation Street being carried on a series of railway bridges that took the road some 25 feet above the tracks.

For the first six months of 1952, the date of the 'past' photograph, the Bristol Road tram services were still operating, and the routes to Rednal, Rubery and Cotteridge terminated next to sets of impressive shelters over one of the railway bridges in the section of Navigation Street between Suffolk Street and Hill Street. Tramcar 518, a Brush-built bogie tramcar of 1913, has just unloaded its passengers, having worked the 70 service from Rednal. The third tram is 1928-built air-braked car 778, and is loading up passengers before leaving on the 71 service to Rubery. In the distance, turning right into John Bright Street, is a two-year-old Crossley-bodied 'new-look'-fronted Crossley DD42/7. Beyond the bus, the steam from a passing locomotive spills over the bridge and partially obscures the grime-covered buildings in Pinfold Street, which carry the advertisement for the very strong Wills's Capstan cigarettes. On the extreme right are the six-storey premises on the corner of Lower Temple Street. What the picture shows is how, in 1952, the smoke-blackened city centre was still at the human-sized scale of development, with nothing dominating the skyline above the level of the Pinfold Street buildings. Within ten years, however, this would change, and later redevelopment in the 1980s would further alter the city skyline dramatically.

The trams went on 5 June 1952 and their passenger shelters were abandoned 20 years later, leaving Navigation Street rather quieter in 1999 than in years gone by. Although still used by buses, it lost its city terminus status in the mid-1980s, when the routes from the south-west were extended into the city centre. A sad loss was the demolition in the late 1960s of the White Swan public house, the site of which is still a car park, from which the silver BMW car is emerging on the right of the 'present' picture. During 2001, work at last began on this 30-odd-year-old car park, with the construction of luxury apartments. Today Navigation Street is dominated by the rather dated concrete New Street Station signal box built in 1965. Described by Nikolaus Pevsner as a 'liquorice allsorts' structure, it is now a listed building. The red-brick premises in Pinfold Street have been restored and cleaned, as have the Italianate-styled premises on the corner of Lower Temple Street and Stephenson Street. In the distance on the extreme right in Navigation Street is the new entrance to New Street Station.

What has changed most is the sheer scale of the distant city centre buildings. The old Theatre Royal in New Street was demolished in 1957 after the last performance of 'The Fol-de-Rols' on 15 December 1956, and with it went the old Colonnade Hotel on the corner of Ethel Street. These were replaced by the Woolworth Building and the much smaller Winston Churchill House. But even this has changed. In the late 1980s, after Woolworth's vacated the premises, the whole structure was extensively expanded – mainly upwards – so that it now dominates the impersonal skyline. *A. Yates/ DRH*

The six-storey buildings on the corner of **LOWER TEMPLE STREET** and **STEPHENSON STREET** formed part of the original 1875 Birmingham Improvement Scheme along New Street and Corporation Street, which included the Midland Hotel, Burlington Arcade and Passage. On 23 June 1954 the block retains all of its original Victorian elegance, with shops such as June Mackay's gown specialists, later to become part of Hudson's bookshops and the baker A. D. Wimbush, while opposite are the dignified car showrooms of Rootes Limited, selling Hillman, Humber, Singer and Sunbeam cars, seemingly fitting comfortably into the 1950s city centre landscape. Car parking in the city centre was not a problem; motorists could almost abandon their cars without a thought of traffic wardens, parking meters or a rush hour exit from the city centre that seemingly lasted for hours. In the 1950s most cars on the road were made in Britain, and this selection of early post-war cars includes, from right to left, a Ford V8 Pilot, a Hillman Minx Phase III, an Austin Princess A135 Mark II, a Vauxhall Wyvern EIX and, on the left, a Hillman Californian coupé. At the top of Lower Temple Street, beyond Burlington Passage, is Day's boot and shoe manufacturers and the stationers H. P. Pope, famous for their illuminated Swan's pens advertisement. Opposite Pope's, in the pinnacled building in New Street, was Paige Gowns, a rather 'superior' ladies' clothes shop.

Although pedestrianised in 1995, Lower Temple Street looks the same as it did nearly 50 years ago, although impressions can be most deceptive. The Victorian block is now just a facade, as in 1997 the whole of the old Midland Hotel premises was gutted internally and rebuilt, and in the process the old Burlington Passage was lost. The site of this former passage entrance is the glass-covered section between the two blocks of buildings to the right of the stainless steel CCTV mast in the foreground. The former car showroom on the left went through a number of metamorphoses, including one selling high-quality hi-fi equipment. Today, like the shop opposite and its predecessor in 1954, the old car showrooms have become a 'designer-wear' clothes shop. The Travel West Midlands Mercedes-Benz 0405 single-decker bus coming along Stephenson Street on the extreme right is displaying the destination M78, the 'M' signifying that it passes a number of the stations on the new Birmingham to Wolverhampton Metro tram line. When the Metro is extended from Snow Hill it will follow Stephenson Street on its way from Corporation Street to Victoria Square. *Birmingham City Engineer & Surveyor's Dept/DRH*

COLMORE ROW has had various names in its history, but originally most of its length was called Ann Street after Ann Colmore, whose family owned the land on the ridge to the north of the growing town and gave the land for St Philip's Church, which was later to become Birmingham Cathedral. The area grew in the early years of the 18th century to become the fashionable location for the stylish residences of leading merchants and the newly wealthy manufacturers. By 1831 the population of Birmingham had reached about 25,000, and with industrial development taking place on all sides, except in the west, the Colmore Estate lands remained the area in which the wealthy people of Birmingham retained their gracious town houses.

Industry brought prosperity; prosperity brought finance and banking; and banking of course brought wealth. But it was wealth at a price! Birmingham's industrial growth in the late 18th and 19th century attracted workers from the surrounding countryside who were pulled into the growing town by the prospect of obtaining their own 'crock of gold'. In 1837, at the outset of Queen Victoria's reign, the population of Birmingham was about 170,000. By 1870 this figure had almost trebled. Unfortunately the infrastructure – water supply, sewage and the municipal planning of the town – did not match this population growth and most of the town was quite squalid.

After 1866, when the leases of the buildings in Ann Street came up for renewal, a start was made on widening the road, and it was renamed Colmore Row. The Georgian terraces were being swept away in about 1875, the date of the first 'past' picture. Already the new premises of the Birmingham District & Counties Bank has been built on the new alignment of Colmore Row, much taller than the doomed houses around it. It was through the vision of Joseph Chamberlain, who became Mayor of the Birmingham Borough Council in 1873, that various revolutionary schemes were instigated, some of which are still evident today in the layout of the city centre.

In the 19th century, the Victorians fly-posted buildings with advertisements for virtually any product, proposed meeting or local event. The exposed wall beyond the new bank bears an advert for something that, although transformed by the passage of time, is still with us today: 'Excursion to Alton Towers – 6s and 3s'. Of course, the Victorians wouldn't be riding on the 'Black Hole', but would be enjoying the more prosaic delights of the arboretum! Other attractions have changed less: there are trips by train to Scarboro' (the spelling on the notice), the Isle of Man, horse-racing at Nottingham and an excursion to Wimbledon. This could have been to visit the All-England Lawn Tennis & Croquet Club, which held its first amateur championship for men in 1877. An important link with Birmingham is that the game of 'tennis-on-the-lawn' was first played on a court in Ampton Road, Edgbaston, by Major Walter Clopton Wingfield, who was the first Wimbledon champion. Beyond the iron railings around St Philip's churchyard on the right is the Blue Coat School's original 1794 building, which was demolished in 1935 when the school moved to new purpose-built premises on the corner of Metchley Lane and Somerset Road, Harborne.

The second view along Colmore Row dates from immediately after the Second World War; the lamp standard on the corner of Colmore Row still displays its wartime blackout markings. The photograph shows that much of the rebuilding from the Joseph Chamberlain era has remained unaltered. The wrought-iron railings around the churchyard succumbed to the publicity drive by Max Aitken (Lord Beaverbrook) for scrap metal, while the Blue Coat School building has been replaced by the rather severe Portland stone-faced Prudential Building. The recent re-enclosure of the Churchyard by the Millennium-inspired wrought-iron railings in 2001 has resulted in a somewhat claustrophobic feel to the area. The old Birmingham District & Counties Bank, the forerunner of Barclays Bank, has extended into the premises next door. Beyond Church Street is the impressive Grand Hotel, designed by Thomson Plevins in 1875. There is only one post-war car in this view, the Staffordshire-registered Austin 10hp on the left. Behind it, still with white-painted wartime bumpers, is a Ford De Luxe Model C, which was also a 10 hp car, and beyond that is a 1933 Wolseley Hornet. On the Cathedral side, the leading car is a 1938 Jowett 10hp, and behind it is a Wolseley 12/48 and a Rover 12 or 14. Just visible behind the Rover are the impressive bus shelters that were some of the few in the city centre to afford the waiting passenger some protection. Beyond Snow Hill Station, in the distant gap in the skyline, is Steelhouse Lane. A totally enclosed bogie tramcar, still in its elaborate pre-war livery, is waiting in Steelhouse Lane outside the Wesleyan & General Building before working on one of the three Erdington routes.

Most of the north side of Colmore Row's Victorian development from Livery Street to Newhall Street has remained intact and has managed to retain much of its original character, largely because it is designated as a preservation area. The facade and splendid banking hall of the old Birmingham District building, designed by Yeoville Thomason, survive, as do the former Barclays Bank and the Grand Hotel beyond Church Street. For the second time in just over a century, Colmore Row was realigned in the 1990s with wider pavements and the dreaded speed-bumps. Fortunately, although many of the buildings now only retain their facades, the street retains the 'human scale' feeling. Coupled with the Churchyard opposite, this tree-lined boulevard is still one of the real unspoilt gems of Birmingham City Centre. *J. Whybrow Collection(2)/DRH*

With the distant columns of the Town Hall marking the far end of **COLMORE ROW**, the early-19th-century Phoenix Assurance building on the corner of Temple Row is about to be closed and replaced by a more modern, Portland stone-faced building. The arrow along the buildings indicates that the company is moving, albeit temporarily, to the new Phoenix Chambers. This four-storey building was designed by G. Thomas and contained the usual banking, insurance and legal advisory companies that had become associated with this prestigious area of Birmingham. The scale of the buildings was,

in the late 19th century, beginning to change from the original Georgian town houses built in Ann Street and subsequently altered to become offices, to the new larger Victorian commercial buildings. What is surprising is the lack of anything really happening in this view of the normally busy Colmore Row. Could it have been a Sunday?

It is also extremely quiet on 19 May 1999, although it is a Wednesday, not a Sunday. In fact, it is just a brief break in the traffic as the last of the cars escapes from Colmore Row into Newhall Street before the traffic lights change to red. The

former Phoenix Assurance building, which had replaced the older premises, still displays the Phoenix bird over the doorway, but the building itself is now occupied by the Chesterton Group. The block beyond Waterloo Passage is now the Birmingham headquarters of the West Bromwich Building Society. Rising above the distant Town Hall is Richard Sieffert's Alpha Tower. The sheer size of this building rather disguises the fact that it is on the other side of Suffolk Street Queensway on the corner of Broad Street. This cantilevered construction of some 30 storeys is being protected at the time of writing as a piece of outstanding early 1970s architecture. *J. Whybrow collection/DRH*

The old hospital buildings on the corner of **STEELHOUSE LANE** and **UPPER PRIORY** had long since lost their medical function by the late 1950s. On 5 August 1959 the building, by now housing the Government's local Fuel Overseer's Office, is in its last throes of occupancy before being swept away in the redevelopment of the area in the early 1960s. Upper Priory got its name from a small chapel and house belonging to an order of Augustinian priors who had become victims of the Dissolution of the Monasteries as late as 1547. The whole area was subsequently developed by a Quaker iron master, one John Pemberton, who bought the abandoned monastery land in 1697, and over the next 30 years redeveloped the Bull Street, Old Square and Upper and Lower Priory areas. The prosperity of the area was maintained until the middle of the 19th century, when encroaching commercial uses as well as small back-yard factories began to encroach upon the area. Nearby Bull Street, on the other hand, became the fashionable shopping street in Regency Birmingham, and this spilled over into Steelhouse Lane. In Upper Priory a new Central Fire Station was built in 1883 on the opposite side to the hospital, and this lasted until it was replaced by the Central Fire Station in Lancaster Place in 1935 as it was 'practically traffic-bound'. As usual, the cars of the day are interesting: the leading one is a virtually brand-new Vauxhall Victor F series Mark II, while behind it is an Austin A40, a Hillman Minx estate and a Morris Minor Traveller. These are parked alongside the shops in Steelhouse Lane that included, on the corner of Bull Street, the shoe shop of Freeman, Hardy & Willis, while catering for the traveller using Birmingham's Snow Hill Station was Griffin's newsagent and two premises belonging to Withers the tobacconist. There is also Lesly's jewellery shop and the furniture 'outpost' of the Bull Street-based department store of Edward Grey. The tall building with the round-topped corner piece belongs to Boots the Chemist and is situated on the corner of Bull Street and Colmore Row.

The present-day view is totally unrecognisable. Looking from in front of the Wesleyan & General Building, it can be seen that Colmore Circus swallowed up most the top end of Steelhouse Lane and the original alignment of Snow Hill. The huge traffic island left beneath it another unfriendly pedestrian underpass with labyrinthine passageways reached only by intimidatingly dark steps and passageways. With vehicles separated from pedestrians in this remnant of 1960s town planning, it leaves even the surrounding buildings seemingly rather perched above the hole in the ground. In 2001 work began to fill in this unsightly and basically useless hole as part of the scheme to take the tracks of the Metro out of the nearby Snow Hill Station and through the city centre, as well as adding new retail and office areas to the site, as seen in the third photograph. Above the road on the left is Dr Johnson House, whose main entrance is in Bull Street. This is the Society of Friends Meeting House and was the successor to the original structure built in 1702. Just visible on the left is the line of the old Upper Priory, which was realigned to form Priory Queensway, and the uninspired former warehouse block for the long-closed Lewis's department store. Dominating the skyline is the blue-and-grey-clad Colmore Gate, opened in 1997. This impressive multi-storey office block tower somehow reflects the 'computer age' in its styling and, of course, with its internal

fixtures. This occupies the site of the former Boots premises on the corner of Colmore Row and Bull Street and represents, with its street-level cafes and bars beneath the offices, the style of structure that was being encouraged in Birmingham in the late 1990s. *Birmingham City Engineer & Surveyor's Dept/DRH*

STEELHOUSE LANE was named after Kettle's Steelhouses, a number of small foundries near Newton Street that were in operation throughout the 18th century. The road came to real prominence in the early 19th century when it briefly became the main routeway from Colmore Row to the north-west towards Aston and eventually Birmingham's diocesan centre at Lichfield. After the 'cutting' of Corporation Street beyond Old Square and the completion of the Victoria Law Courts by 1891, despite its slower development than the first section from New Street, Steelhouse Lane's commercial development went into decline. The less impressive rear elevation of the Law Courts was built beyond Newton Street and is visible as the first imposing building beyond the cars on the right. At the bottom of Steelhouse Lane is the Central Police Station, which can be distinguished by its plethora of tall chimneys. Opposite it is the General Hospital, opened in 1897 to replace an older Georgian structure. The shops on the left of Steelhouse Lane include Frank Hammond's second-hand-book shop, which in the mid-1960s was a wonderful emporium for purchasing redundant library books. Beyond are the premises of W. Pond & Co Ltd, suppliers of every sort of tools from saws and chisels to the latest Wolf power drills – a predecessor of today's more common Black & Decker. Pond's other peculiar claim to fame was that they advertised their shop under the title 'Pond For Tools' on the balcony ends of a select few of Birmingham's tramcar fleet.

With the snow still on the roofs in this gloomy 5 February 1954 view, the lights are switched on in the offices of H. Wiggins on the right. The parked cars include a 1946-registered Austin 10, a Rover 75 and, outside Pond's, an Austin A40 10 cwt van, a Morris Minor, a Vauxhall 14hp J-type, a Hillman Husky and a very old Ford Popular Y-type dating from about 1934. On the right is another Morris Minor, a Coventry-registered 1937 Rover 12 and a Humber Hawk IV. Any evidence of the recently departed tramcars has virtually gone, although the last tram services had run here only seven months earlier on 4 July 1953, after which the tracks were lifted and the road resurfaced. Careful examination of the lamp standard on the left reveals the remnants of a bracket arm just below the lamp, while just above the Rover is one of those strange junction boxes that were attached to some traction poles.

The truncated and somewhat emasculated Steelhouse Lane is viewed from the *Birmingham Post & Mail* building in Colmore Circus in 2002, and it can be seen just how much its importance has diminished over the years. It wasn't so long ago when this was one of the major roads leading from the city centre into Lancaster Place, but for many years the traffic flow was reversed so that vehicles could only come up from 'Hawkins Corner' at the bottom of Corporation Street, passing the Diana, Princess of Wales Children's Hospital on their right. In 2002, as part of the Masshouse Circus diversions, traffic was going down Steelhouse Lane again, albeit only as far as Printing House Street. At the bottom of Steelhouse Lane is the back of the Victoria Law Courts. Beyond the corner of Coleridge Passage are the old 1890s cell blocks and towards the bottom of Steelhouse Lane is the Central Police Station. On the right is the early 1960s Priory House, built on the site of the old town Fire Station. *Birmingham City Engineer & Surveyor's Dept/DRH*

Bennetts Hill was first laid out with houses in 1827, although the road had been in existence since before the Napoleonic Wars, being named after the Bennett family who had farmed this part of the Colmore Estate. Near the still extant Regency houses lining the hill from Colmore Row is **WATERLOO STREET**. This is a continuation of Temple Street, which skirts around the edge of St Philip's Cathedral churchyard and bisects Bennetts Hill. Waterloo Street was obviously named after the successful battle of 18 June 1815 in Belgium, when the Napoleonic forces were defeated. When it was first built it was observed to be 'a new improvement to the town' with its tastefully designed houses. On the corner of Waterloo Street and Bennetts Hill stands the building originally constructed in 1833 for the National Provincial Bank. It was rebuilt in 1869 by John Gibson to a large-windowed Corinthian-order pattern, and in this style it survived as a bank until well into the 1990s. In May 1970, the date of the 'past' picture, the bank is still suffering from an identity crisis as it still displays over the revolving door in the porch the name of its first owner, but the two nameplates on either side of the main entrance reveal that it is by now part of the National Westminster Bank. The one-way traffic flow along Waterloo Street is directed towards Victoria Square, and an Austin 1100, a 1965-registered Jaguar E Type, a Ford Anglia Estate and a Morris 1800, affectionately remembered as a 'land-crab', are parked at the newly installed parking meters outside the bank, with a nearly new Ford Cortina parked on the right. The seven-storey building is the 1930s Neville House, which contained the offices of various solicitors, accountants and insurance companies.

Today the buildings all remain intact as part of the Waterloo Street conservation area, but closer examination reveals dramatically altered usage to meet the demands of the present day. The former National Provincial Bank is now Bennetts Wine Bar and serves a professional clientele that during the day is perhaps not so different from 30 years earlier. The giant Corinthian columns and the semi-circular-topped windows of the original banking hall are complemented by the domed corner entrance over which stands the City Coat of Arms and various devises to represent Birmingham's range of industry. The traffic flow in Waterloo Street has been reversed in conjunction with the removal of vehicular traffic from Victoria Square, but in essence the street remains, externally at least, largely unaltered from the previous photograph, as a small island of charming Regency buildings. Even the rather ugly Neville House has a certain dated inter-war charm, despite its uninspired rectangular frontage. *Birmingham Public Works Department/DRH*

It was only very rarely that a Birmingham City Transport bus strayed off its normal route, so the reason why one is coming down **BENNETTS HILL** from Colmore Row towards New Street is now lost in the 'mists of time'. It is about 1957 and the bus, 2153 (JOJ 153), a 1949 Leyland 'Titan' PD2/1 with a Leyland 54-seater body, is working on a 15B service to Whittington Oval in Yardley. It is about to cross the junction where Bennetts Hill intersects Waterloo Street. The triangular area between Colmore Row and New Street, which at first had Christ Church at its apex, was one of the final parts of central Birmingham to be freshly built upon, leaving just the area to the east, around St Philip's, to remain as what turned out to be the last area of open space in the middle of the town. The Royal Insurance Company occupied No 7 Bennetts Hill, on the left-hand corner of Waterloo Street. This was built on the site of the News Room of 1825 and dates from about the 1870s. Opposite, at 34-36 Bennetts Hill, is the five-storey London Assurance Building, constructed in 1909 to the design of Leonard Stokes, and although its arched ground-floor windows have been altered, the simple stone-clad nature of the original design remains an interesting contrast with the buildings in the rest of the street. Behind the bus and the Bradford van, on the far corner of Colmore Row, is the old Union Club building designed in 1869 by Yeoville Thomason.

The most delightful Regency houses to survive in the centre of the city are in Bennetts Hill. From the corner of Colmore Row, Nos 1 to 5, seen in the first 1999 view, comprise a set of two-bay houses with beautifully symmetrical round-headed doorways. These five houses were built in 1827 and represent the earliest development in Bennetts Hill. They were probably

designed by Charles Edge, who was later to design the Market Hall in the Bull Ring and be responsible for the completion of the Town Hall. On the extreme left, one building away from the corner of Waterloo Street, is a Regency house of a different style, which has survived the developments in this commercial hub of the city. These buildings have taken on a new secure lease of life in the Waterloo Street Conservation Area, despite being only the facades of the original structures. Rising behind them, in Colmore Row, is the National Westminster Bank tower, dating from the early 1990s and which, despite its size, has a certain pleasing symmetry that does not look too out of place when compared to the 19th-century buildings standing below it on the southern side of Colmore Row.

Although only distantly seen behind the bus in the 1957 photograph of Bennetts Hill, the Bamford Trust premises on the corner of Newhall Street is one of Yeoville Thomason's finest city centre buildings. Seen in the third view on a sunny day in September 1999, the grace of this fine Victorian building can be appreciated. Built as the Renaissance Union Club in 1869, it has a formalised Corinthian-capitalled entrance and subtly pedimented windows on the first floor above a decorative balustraded cornice. Beyond is the Royal Bank of Scotland's building, also designed by Thomason and, like the old Union Club, now a Grade II listed building. This is despite having been hugely expanded in the last years of the 20th century by having additional storeys built above the Victorian roof-line. What is pleasing is that these buildings have survived in Colmore Row and have not been swept away in the carnage that so badly afflicted so much of the rest of the city centre! *R. F. Mack/DRH (2)*

NEWHALL STREET was built on the line of the trees flanking the main drive to the Colmore family home at New Hall, which stood at the present-day junction of Great Charles Street and Newhall Street, very much in the area where this photograph was taken in the summer of 1972. The hall was pulled down in 1787, but the earlier Georgian development in Colmore Row opposite St Philip's Church had really not taken over much of the land being sold on leases by the Colmore family. The result was that much of the development in the section of Newhall Street between Great Charles Street and Cornwall Street did not start to take place for another 80 or so years, as it lay away from the already thriving commercial 'heartland' in Colmore Row, Ann Street and, a little later, around Bennetts Hill. The banks and the larger financial institutions tended to occupy the larger premises nearer the town centre, while the smaller legal and financial services were clustered more peripherally in streets such as Newhall Street and Cornwall Street.

Newhall Street was eventually occupied by three distinct and differently styled office premises, and in 1972 this flurry of commercial growth still retained its original 'professional' occupations. On the corner, at No 61, with its Tudor-style leaded-window bays, are the solicitors Grey and Willcox. Occupying the ground floor of Avebury House, at 55-59, is, appropriately, The Solicitors' Law Stationery Society Ltd. Avebury House was built in 1911 around a steel frame, masked by some classical detail such as the vestige of a pediment and the corner pilasters, and is the home almost exclusively of accountants and solicitors who occupied the smaller offices that proliferated in this part of the Edwardian city. Next to it is the earlier Cornwall Buildings of about 1898, containing the offices of similar professionals and displaying all the architectural characteristics of the Arts and Crafts revival, being built in red brick with terracotta relief coupled to Dutch-styled ogee gables. Just peeking over the roofs is a sign of things to come, with 1960s multi-storey office blocks occupying sites in Great Charles Street, Edmund Street and Church Street.

Yet again, in the commercial centre of Birmingham, if the buildings haven't been replaced, then at least most of their original use has migrated away to more prestigious city-centre office suites or they have just been vacated for cheaper suburban offices. Strangely, the middle of Birmingham is still called the 'town centre' by locals, despite it having been a city for 110 years. The Grey and Willcox offices have been empty for a number of years, while The Solicitors' Law Stationery Society has become the Simply Blue Restaurant and the corner ground-floor of Cornwall Buildings has become the Cornwall Wine Bar. There are still solicitors, lawyers and accountants using the upper storeys of these premises, but there is a definite move away from these fortunately listed buildings to more user- and computer-friendly purpose-built offices. At one time, at 5.00pm, when the offices shut, this part of the city closed down. Today, parts of Newhall Street, Cornwall Street and Church Street are left to the tender mercies of the daytime wine bars and the city nightlife.

One of the hazards of taking 'past and present' photographs is the unexpected. This occurred on 5 September 1999, which with positively beautiful weather conditions and plenty of time appeared to be a perfect opportunity. Being a Sunday, with not too much traffic ready to 'mow down' the intrepid photographer standing in the middle of a road with his back to the traffic, all seemed well. Unfortunately, the junction was being resurfaced, so temporary traffic lights scattered around the junction didn't exactly help, nor did the asphalt lorry parked right outside the main subject of the photograph! *Birmingham Public Works Department/DRH*

ECCLESIASTICAL

The original Christian church in Birmingham was roughly on the site of the present St Martin's Parish Church in the Bull Ring. The first mention of a church at this location was in 1263, though there had almost certainly been a church here at the time of the Domesday Book of 1086. The mother church of Birmingham stood at the centre of routeways, near the market and therefore at the focus of trade. The original sandstone church was much rebuilt over the succeeding centuries, but it gradually fell into what was described as a 'pitiful state'. The present 14th-century-Gothic-style church of St Martin was completed in 1875 to the designs of J. A. Chatwin, and its position at the heart of the city survived severe damage in the air-raid of 10 April 1941, but not the ripping out of the church's heartland when the Bull Ring was redeveloped during the 1960s. Present-day plans for the redevelopment of the whole of the Bull Ring area are due for completion in the first decade of the century and this will hopefully restore the church's traditional hinterland between it and High Street.

After the Civil War and the religious upheavals of the Stuarts, the need for a new church at 'the top of the town' became essential, although one must suspect that the Colmore and Newhall families had their new church built so that they did not have to mix with what another son of Birmingham, Tony Hancock, once described as 'the hoi polloi' of the 'rough end' of the town. The attractive town houses built over the next century, coupled with the efforts of protective estate landowners, managed to keep the industry of the 18th century at bay. The new church was St Philip's, designed by Thomas Archer in an English Baroque style and consecrated, although without its tower, in 1715; the tower was added ten years later. In 1884 the church was extended with the addition of a chancel, designed to match the Baroque style by J. A. Chatwin, who only 11 years earlier had been responsible for the effectively new St Martin's Parish Church, designed in the totally different Gothic style. In 1905 St Philip's became the Church of England Cathedral of the newly created Diocese of Birmingham. Unlike the Parish Church, surrounded by market bustle and traffic, the Cathedral stands in what is known simply as 'The Churchyard'. This area of trees and elaborate tombstones has for many years been a haven for peace and quiet, only spoiled, especially at dusk, by large numbers of pigeons, despite efforts to cull them.

The Jewish and Roman Catholic communities were traditionally smaller in Birmingham than in other comparable English towns in the 19th century. The Jewish community made little or no impact on the area covered by this book, with their places of worship being built outside what is now the Queensway Inner Ring Road, although the first synagogue was actually in Severn Street. A new, large synagogue was built in Blucher Street, behind Holloway Head, and was one of the earliest commissions of the architect Yeoville Thomason, who was later responsible for the design of the Council House. The synagogue was built in 1856 in an Italianate, red-brick style with attractive light stonework dressings. In the mid-1930s a new synagogue was built in Sheepcote Street, at the top of Broad Street.

Catholic churches were also something of a rarity, the chapel of St Peter, in St Peter's Place, being one of the first post-Reformation Roman Catholic churches to be built in the town. It was consecrated in 1786 and was deliberately built in plain brick to look at first sight like a warehouse, because even in Birmingham, where free speech and free religious expression were encouraged, it was still dangerous to be a practising Catholic. The brick-built Roman Catholic Cathedral of St Chad was built between 1839 and 1856, although, with the exception of the west tower, it was effectively finished in 1841. It was designed by A. W. N. Pugin and stood among the late-Georgian houses and workshops of the gun trade area, similar to a French Cathedral emerging from the side streets of a medieval town. This was somewhat contrary, as the style chosen by Pugin was distinctly north German!

While the Church of England was important, it

was the nonconformists and dissenters who were frequently the driving force in the town. Presbyterians in Graham Street in 1824, Congregationalists in Carrs Lane in their rebuilt chapel in 1820, Quakers in Bull Street, and Unitarians in Broad Street in 1862 were just some of the nonconformist groups that thrived in the 18th and 19th centuries in Birmingham, and whose religious and architectural legacy is still with us today.

The increasing redevelopment of the town throughout the Victorian period began with the demolition of two chapels, one in King Street and another, Lady Huntington's Chapel, in Peck Lane, and the removal of bodies from a cemetery in 1849 in preparation for the construction of the London & North Western Railway's New Street Station, which saw its first train on 1 July 1852. In the 1880s, with the enlargement of the station by the Midland Railway on the Dudley Street side, there was the loss in Meeting Street of a Unitarian Chapel. The continued enlargement and increasing prosperity of Birmingham culminated in the granting of city status in 1889, while the next major event was the creation of the Church of England Diocese of Birmingham in 1905 and the upgrading of St Philip's into a Cathedral. This was the high point of church development in the city centre, as redevelopment and commercial considerations resulted in the selling off for property development of many of the small chapels dotted around the inner area, such as that in Lower Priory, the attractively towered church of Bishop Ryder in Gem Street, St Jude's in Hill Street and, of course, the much larger, death-watch-beetle-infested Christ Church. During the bombing of the Second World War, although a number of the remaining churches received bomb damage, the worst casualty was in Bath Row, just outside the geographical boundary of this book, where the splendid Regency church of St Thomas, with its Ionic-columned portico, was destroyed.

The post-war immigration into Birmingham of people of the Muslim, Sikh and Buddhist faiths had little effect on the city centre, as by the mid-1950s, despite the city becoming a multi-faith and multi-cultural city, the new God of Mammon or its new mobile equivalent, the motorcar, with its all-pervasive need for more and more roads, had taken over all the available space, so that the requirements of these additional faiths were eventually met by the construction of new temples and places of worship well beyond even the fringes of the city centre. The Central Mosque, an ornate building on the site of the long-closed Dares Brewery, had to be constructed in 1989 on the distant Belgrave Middleway, which is about 2 miles from the city centre. Even St Chad's Roman Catholic Cathedral of 1841 has to be construed as being at the margins of the present-day city centre.

Those churches that have survived into the 21st century have thrived, although over the years the Cathedral churchyard area in Colmore Row has had to defend its sanctity against proposals to shave part of it away in order to accommodate an aborted scheme to make Colmore Row a dual-carriageway section of the Inner Ring Road. In the Bull Ring, the hinterland of St Martin's has been reduced to the extent that the city's Parish Church is little more than an ecclesiastical island. A lot has been lost, but fortunately there are still a few havens of peace and tranquillity left in the bustling city centre of Birmingham.

Overleaf The Parish Church of Birmingham is the long-established **ST MARTIN'S-IN-THE-BULL RING**. A church has stood on or near this site since before the Domesday Book of 1086, when the Lord of the Manor's land was worth 20 shillings and supported a population of barely 60 people.

Birmingham grew up around the crossing point of the River Rea in what is now Digbeth. There were good-quality water meadows that provided fertile soils, low surrounding hills with heathland suitable for grazing animals, and deciduous woodland, which was part of the then extensive Forest of Arden, supplying materials for fuel and construction. The Lord of the Manor set up his fortified house on one of the northern river terraces of the Rea around the present-day site of Smithfield Market in Moat Row. The church for this early settlement was built halfway up the hill in the 12th century, and around it grew up the market, the Royal Charter for which was granted to Peter, the Lord of Birmingham, in about 1150 by King Henry II. By the late 13th century a larger sandstone church had been built by the de Bermingham family, and in 1690 this medieval building was encased in brick because it had weathered so badly. In 1853 the present-day tower and spire was built to the designs of P. C. Hardwick, as not enough money had been raised in the town to

completely rebuild the church. Nearly 20 years later the nave and the aisles were in such a ruinous state that they were in need of urgent replacement. The cost was £32,000, and despite the fact that only half of this was raised, demolition began in 1873.

A completely new structure, based on the medieval foundations, was built to the design of Julius Alfred Chatwin. He was a prolific, locally based designer of Gothic-styled churches and Renaissance-styled secular buildings, and he produced an attractive, well-proportioned church in the 14th-century Gothic style, which enlarged the medieval ground plan considerably at the eastern end. The combination of his 1875 body of the church and the 1855 tower, plus a few remnants of the medieval church such as the floor tiles and some of the lower masonry in the nave and the tower, is what has survived to the present day. The new Parish Church of St Martin was consecrated on 20 July 1875 by the Bishop of Worcester.

The Bull Ring area was dominated by the Victorian Parish Church. This 1950s 'past' view, best dated by the age of the Midland Red buses parked alongside the shelters beneath the trees in front of the church, shows the large open space that held the daily open-air market. Behind the church to the right is Spiceal Street, whose name reflects the linen and silk merchants who were based there in medieval times. The tall gabled building with the turret on the corner is the impressive-looking St Martin's Hotel. This view was taken from the corner of Charles Edge's splendid Doric-porched Market Hall, opened on Thursday 12 February 1835 and demolished in 1962. Just visible on the right is the sign for Bell Street; this was mounted

on the wall of Birmingham's Fish Market, which had a reputation for being the best inland fresh fish market in England. There are a few barrows selling fruit and vegetables, which have attracted the people on the right, but the majority of the gathered crowd are standing listening to various soap-box orators at Birmingham's equivalent of London's Speakers Corner at Hyde Park. Just above the circle of intently listening folk is the statue of Admiral Horatio Nelson. This was unveiled on 25 October 1809, and although it was one of the smallest erected to the memory of the victor of the battles of Aboukir Bay, Copenhagen and Trafalgar, it had the distinction of being the first in the country, predating Nelson's Column in London by more than 30 years.

The steepness of the Bull Ring as it climbs from Digbeth can best be judged by the roof-line of the buildings on the left going towards the Royal George public house on the corner of Park Street. The row of shop fronts behind Nelson's statue were occupied by the rather faded premises of Oswald Bailey's Army and Navy Stores until their demolition in 1961. A policeman on point duty has stopped the cars – led by a pre-war Humber Super Snipe saloon – coming down the Bull Ring from High Street, in order to allow traffic to follow the tram tracks into Moor Street. What is strange is that the only car coming into the city, a Fiat 500 'Topolino', appears to be intent on going straight up the Bull Ring towards High Street and New Street. One of the forgotten features of the old Bull Ring was that it had a road surface of wooden blocks, which were lethal in icy and wet weather conditions.

Since 1962 St Martin's-in-the Bull Ring has stood facing a huge hole in the ground, when the last vestiges of the hill up to the top of the Bull Ring were excavated to form St Martin's Circus. While the church has remained largely untouched, all around it has been dramatically altered. Ironically, the Bull Ring is due for another renewal barely 40 years after the last attempt at urban redevelopment.

The design for an Inner Ring Road around the city centre had been first proposed in 1917, and a similar concept was approved by the City Council in July 1944. The scheme, to the designs of Herbert Manzoni, was intended to take vehicles around the city centre, rather than through the ever-increasing congestion of the centre. The main flaw in the basic concept was that at the seven main junctions, of which St Martin's Circus was one, the traffic movement was controlled by gyratory systems, coyly named 'Circuses'. The Ministry of Transport finally gave its approval on 18 January 1957 and work began on the first phase around the Horse Fair and Smallbrook Street in March of that year. The second section, around the Bull Ring, was begun in 1960 and was substantially completed by 1964. The lovely old Market Hall was needlessly pulled down, which was a great disappointment, as one of the earlier proposals had retained this splendid building. Most of Spiceal Street, including the branch of F. W. Woolworth that had a most wonderful creaking wooden floor, was also demolished. The

Bull Ring itself was dissected by the part of the Inner Ring Road known as St Martin's Circus. The plan was to segregate traffic from pedestrians, and it certainly succeeded, although it was the car that dominated, leaving the poor old pedestrians to gain access to the Bull Ring by way of subterranean passages. There was even Europe's first open-air escalator to take market-searching folk into a troglodyte routeway of labyrinthine proportions before emerging in the open-air market, which was surrounded by roads circulating at the proper ground level some 30 feet above! Alongside the market was another first: the Bull Ring Shopping Centre claimed to be the first indoor shopping centre outside North America. Covering a site of 23 acres, it was fully enclosed with more than 350,000 square feet of shopping space. It was built by John Laing to the designs of Greenwood and Hirst; work began in the middle of 1961 and it was officially opened by HRH The Duke of Edinburgh on 29 May 1964.

The covers of some of the outdoor stalls in front of St Martin's Church can just be seen beyond the concrete bridge at the top of the Bull Ring in the second photograph, dated 1999. A Travel

West Midlands Leyland 'Lynx' single-decker has just climbed up the remnants of the hill from Digbeth and is about to turn into St Martin's Circus. In the foreground can be seen some of the open-air market stalls that stand at the centre of 'the Circus'. Fortunately, this experiment in town planning, which removed so much of the historic Bull Ring hill, has been swept away; by June 2002, as seen in the third view, the spire of St Martin's was framed by the development of the new Bull Ring Centre and the as yet unnamed concourse leading from High Street towards the Parish Church, leaving pedestrians once more able to walk up the Bull Ring from the church into New Street and High Street, passing the new Selfridge's department store on their way. So what about St Martin's-in-the Bull Ring? It has been modernised 'around the edges', with the addition of a parish hall, but is surprisingly intact and unaltered since it was rebuilt following bomb damage. The windows by Burne-Jones are quite splendid, while a number of the medieval sarcophagi remain as a reminder of the church's historic importance to the City of Birmingham. *Author's collection/DRH*

ST PHILIP'S CHURCH was designed by Thomas Archer in 1709. Archer had been a pupil of Sir Christopher Wren and was commissioned by the Colmore family to produce a church suitable for the wealthier inhabitants of Birmingham. His Baroque-style building was substantially completed in 1715, when it was consecrated, although the domed tower was not finished for another ten years. Archer was a 'gentleman architect' whose own estate was in Umberslade in Warwickshire and it was from there that the stone was quarried for the church. Archer had studied architecture in Italy, France and Austria and this, his first commission, was probably his simplest and his best. The site of the new church, on the ridge that Colmore Row traverses, was well above the industrial excesses of the nearby Rea, Hockley Brook and Aston Brook valleys. It was an area where the merchants and iron masters lived in their newly built Georgian town houses, so the new church of St Philip attracted the upper echelons of Birmingham's nouveau riche.

ST. PHILLIP'S CHURCH AND COLMORE ROW, BIRMINGHAM.

Birmingham was transferred from the Lichfield diocese to Worcester in the 1830s, and for the rest of the century it became obvious that the rapidly enlarging town required its own diocese. In the first years of the 20th century, Bishop Charles Gore of Worcester utilised a large anonymous legacy and some of his own personal wealth to back a Bishopric Bill through the House of Commons, supported politically by Sir Joseph Chamberlain. In 1905 St Philip's became the Birmingham Diocese Cathedral Church and Gore became the first Bishop of Birmingham.

In the early 1920s, the date of the 'past' photograph, an open-balconied bogie tramcar, working on the 25 service to Lozells by way of Hamstead Road and Wheeler Street, stands at the Colmore Row terminus shelters alongside the churchyard of the Cathedral. The trams were taken out of this part of Colmore Row on 4 June 1933 when they began operating from a new terminus outside Snow Hill Station, and the 25 route was abandoned not long afterwards on 7 August 1933. The Cathedral stands in its own tree-lined churchyard, which at that time was surrounded by impressive Victorian iron railings. In the background, behind the tramcar, is the old Blue Coat School premises, contemporary with St Philips, having been opened in 1724. The replacement building would be the Portland stone-faced Prudential Buildings.

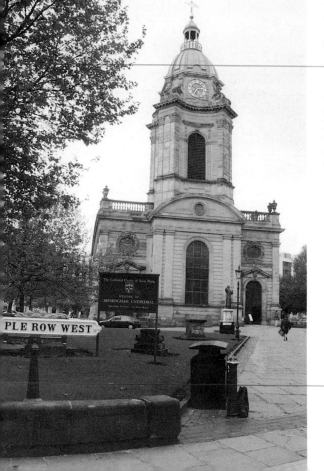

Viewed from Temple Row West in 2000, just before the Millennium railings were erected, the cleaned and renovated St Philip's Cathedral stands in its churchyard, a large open space that has served the city as a quiet oasis amidst the hustle and bustle of the surrounding streets. For many years it also served as a roosting area for the starlings that arrived in huge flocks at dusk, but in recent years they have been largely ousted by pigeons. The simplicity of Thomas Archer's design has survived largely unaltered, to be regarded as one of England's outstanding examples of Queen Anne Baroque architecture. Nearby, the 'cathedral' of the Jewellery Quarter, the beautifully sparse Georgian church of St Paul, built in 1779, displays a similar purposeful style. *Commercial postcard/DRH*

ST PHILIP'S CATHEDRAL CHURCHYARD is not just any churchyard, being known to the citizens of Birmingham as *The* Churchyard. For at least 200 years it has remained a large open space that has managed to both remain as a quiet haven within the busy city centre and retain its religious links with its monuments, obelisks and memorials. By 1953 the Victorian railings in Colmore Row and here in Temple Street were little more than cruelly amputated stumps as a result of the somewhat dubious wartime scrap metal drive. The pathway marks the entrance to the churchyard from Temple Street, which as recently as the early years of this century was gated. On the left is the obelisk memorial to Lt-Col Thomas Unett, born in Birmingham on

12 November 1800 and mortally wounded on 8 September 1855 when commanding the 19th Foot at the siege of Sebastopol. He also saw service at the battles of Alma and Inkerman. The urn-like memorial on the right is to the memory of the Bradam family, while the white obelisk commemorates battles at Khwa in 1875 and Abuklea in 1885. Through the leafless trees is the Prudential Building of 1935, while on the right is the Bank of England, designed by William Doubleday in 1887 and demolished somewhat unnecessarily in 1972. The rather dented rear end of the Bournemouth-registered Austin A70 Hampshire on the right and the pre-war Rover on the left act as 'bookends' to this evocatively bleak November scene.

Today, the churchyard around St Philip's Cathedral looks at first sight much the same. The Unett monument and the white obelisk to the Indian Wars remain, but on this wet May day in 1999 the overall effect is strangely sanitised when compared to the scene 46 years earlier. A danger in compiling any 'Past and Present' volume is viewing the past through rose-coloured glasses. In many ways Birmingham's city centre has benefited from conservation, restoration and even renewal. The brooding presence of Colmore Gate on the distant skyline is a good example of a 1990s development that 'works' quite well, being modern, colourful and bold, even if perhaps rather too dominating so near to the city centre. Contrasting this is the mid-1970s building that replaced the old Bank of England premises, which already looks dated and was ready for the impending redevelopment for the Royal Bank of Scotland in 2001. The Churchyard is now an area of greenery, rather than arboreal restfulness, a feeling of parkland in the middle of the city, which, although most welcome, is in many ways less attractive for being landscaped. *Birmingham City Engineer & Surveyor's Dept/DRH*

The frontages of the buildings on the corner of Moor Street and **NEW MEETING STREET** completely hid the Catholic Church of St Michael. On the left, in the first 'past' picture from 1950, is one of the many run-down buildings in the area that were demolished in the early 1960s; had they survived for a few more years they might well have escaped destruction. This is Dingley's Hotel, dating from the reign of George II, which was pulled down in 1962 to make room for the pavement of the Moor Street Queensway. The large pilasters over the windows and the attractive Doric-arched porch give the building an almost Baroque look, which could be found elsewhere in the Georgian town in Old Square and of course in the influentially styled St Philip's Church. To the left of the approaching trolleybus is the entrance to New Meeting Street, and the premises on which the street name is mounted belong to Messrs Bradford & Fairfax, who were wholesale warehousemen. Although hidden by the trolleybus, the building next door was the Salvation Army Hostel on the corner of Albert Street. The trolleybus is one of the 50 six-wheelers bought by Birmingham Corporation in 1934 for the conversion of the Coventry Road tram route. No 62 (OC 1162), a somewhat dented Metro-Cammell-bodied Leyland TTBD2, is working on the short working service 56 to Hay Mills. By contrast, the almost new Austin Devon already looks dated, as its streamlined shape was first seen in about 1939 on cars being produced in the USA by General Motors.

Moor Street seemed to manage to keep its alleyways far longer than other city centre streets. Narrow streets such as Henns Walk, Shut Lane, Paternoster Row and Scotland Passage, together with New Meeting Street, were lined with warehouses and the backs of premises whose frontages were on more prestigious streets. In the second undated 'past' view in Moor Street, to the right of the 1947 993cc-engined Ford Anglia 8hp EO4A is Bedford & Fairfax's warehouse, while the building on the corner of New Meeting Street, with the

castellated presbytery, belongs to St Michael's. Well hidden from the main road is the church itself, standing in front of a small square. Its Georgian origins are apparently at odds with its denomination, but its sale to the Roman Catholic Church in the 1860s, as recounted on page 41, accounts for this quite rare ecumenical 'take-over'.

The blue plaque on the wall of St Michael's Church, seen in 2000, harks back to the events of the 14 July 1791. Joseph Priestley was due to celebrate the second anniversary of the Storming of the Bastille, one of the first acts of the French Revolution, at a dinner for about 80 of the town's Unitarians and free-thinkers, some of whom were members of the famous Lunar Society. Many townspeople were against Priestley's actions and his anti-Royalist views, and despite their poverty a mob of staunch Royalists stormed Dadley's Hotel; being unable to find Priestley there, they turned their ire on the Unitarians' New Meeting House and burned it down, also destroying its large theological library. It is hard to image today that as a result of the events in this quiet backwater for the next five days the raging mob caused many thousands of pounds worth of damage in the town. Three Unitarian meeting houses were destroyed together with a Baptist church and the houses of a dozen or so dissenters, including William Hutton and Joseph Priestley. Priestley, as well as being the minister of the Unitarian meeting house, was also the father of modern chemistry, having discovered oxygen, ammonia, sulphuric acid and nitrogen. The combustible nature of these discoveries was perhaps not lost on him as he watched his chapel and house go up in smoke. Beyond the church are the steel fire escapes at the rear of the buildings in Albert Street, which look as though they might be more at home in the back alleyways of New York rather than standing opposite a small area of grass, trees and benches, hidden from view in front of Carrs Lane Congregation Church. *A. B. Cross/Birmingham City Engineer & Surveyor's Dept/DRH*

The forgotten architectural gem of **ST MICHAEL'S ROMAN CATHOLIC CHURCH** has an interesting history. It was built in 1802 as a Nonconformist Chapel for the Unitarian Church, to replace the building burned down in the so-called Priestley riots of 1791. It is a rectangular building with a pedimented facade and four sets of paired Ionic pilasters standing above a porticoed entrance hall, reached by a flight of steps. It was built with a galleried interior, reflecting the style of the religious meetings for which it was built. The Unitarians were an influential Nonconformist sect in Birmingham, whose Victorian philanthropic, social and community work, undertaken by influential families such as the Chamberlains, Kenricks, Martineaus and Rylands, became legendary in the town. A slightly later building, just around the corner, was the Carrs Lane Congregational Church, built in 1820, which attracted a similar type of congregation and to some extent made the New Meeting Street building redundant. Partly as a result of this, the Chapel went from one end of the Christian spectrum to the other, being sold in the 1860s to the Roman Catholic Church.

As St Michael's, it survived the demolition of the buildings that stood between it and Moor Street, and after years of being hidden away, its simple Georgian facade is now thrust forward to the wide walkway that runs parallel to Moor Street Queensway. The entrance steps have given way to a raised pavement and the triple porch entrance has been glazed and a new entrance built in the very truncated New Meeting Street. More than 200 years after the Priestley riots the building is now probably as safe as it has ever been, having narrowly escaped the 'let's pull it down if it's old' school of town planning that so decimated Birmingham's city centre in the 1960s and 1970s. On the right are the new student residential

blocks on the Aston University campus, and in the distance the pavement leads down to pedestrian underpasses at the bottom of Albert Street, which for over 40 years left a once thriving area of the city to decay among the stilts of the under-Queensway car parks. Fortunately, in December 1999 a huge development plan was announced that would involve the complete demolition of Masshouse Circus; the cost of this, together with rebuilding and the creation of a new access road, will be £30m, and it will be an integral part of the 'Eastside' development scheme, which will link the £113 million Millennium Point, the 'high-tech' Science Museum development opposite the old Curzon Street Station building, with the redeveloped Bull Ring scheme. The scheme, begun in 2002, will include, for the first time in over a century, the creation of a new area of parkland and tree-lined canal walkways. *Birmingham City Engineer & Surveyor's Dept/DRH*

The tall tower in the background of this snowy view of the northern end of Corporation Street belongs to the METHODIST CENTRAL HALL, constructed in 1903. This section of Chamberlain's 'Parisian boulevard' had only been developed at the turn of the century due to a general downturn in the national economy, which had rather left his 'grand scheme' to peter out before reaching its intended northern destination at Aston Road.

The Second World War is barely six months old and the 'Phoney War' period is having a lesser effect than expected, so life is apparently going on fairly normally as, after a heavy snowfall in February 1940, Birmingham's first tramcar, No 1, travels through the island in Central Place. Close examination shows that beneath the front dash panels the tram has had its lifeguards removed and a snowplough substituted. Of these original 20 tramcars, built in 1904 as open-top bogie cars by ER&TCW, only the first three were equipped with snow ploughs. This tram was to enjoy only another 14 months in service before being destroyed by an oil bomb that hit Miller Street depot in April 1941. It is working on the 6 service into the city and is crossing Central Place before passing into Stafford Street, which is marked by the gap in the buildings on the left. Coming out of the city centre, having travelled down Corporation Street, is 1936 Midland Red double-decker BHA 367, an SOS FEDD with a front-entrance Metro-Cammell body that would eventually receive the fleet number 1822. The unidentified totally enclosed bogie tram crossing Corporation Street is travelling towards its Steelhouse Lane terminus, having worked one of the Erdington group services. Just visible is the trolleybus overhead for the Nechells route, which was abandoned in curious circumstances at the end of September 1940.

Today the northern end of Corporation Street is dominated by two important buildings. Out of sight on the right is the Victoria Law Courts, while opposite is the equally impressive Methodist Central Hall of 1903, designed by E. and J. A. Harper and among the last 'stylish' buildings erected in Corporation Street. All the buildings to the north of the Central Hall were demolished when Masshouse Queensway, just visible to the left, was constructed. This left Corporation Street somewhat truncated, with 'Hawkins Corner' surviving as the 'tailpiece' building carried round into Steelhouse Lane. The Methodist Central Hall is built of red brick and terracotta in a 12-bay design, and is characterised by having octagonal corner turrets and a decorative parapet at roof level. The thin, delicate tower is placed asymmetrically some seven bays from the southern end, and is perhaps the only clue to the building's real purpose. It has shops on the ground floor, which further disguises its ecclesiastical function. Inside, this huge building has a quite lovely main hall that reflects the Art Nouveau architectural embellishments of the early years of the 20th century. Today this part of Corporation Street is as prosperous as it has ever been, having experienced something of a renaissance in the early 1990s. It now includes numerous wine bars and cafes, which cater for both the day-time 'business' trade and the evening nightlife. It is just a pity that Corporation Street has such a disappointing northern end, resembling a suburban cul-de-sac rather than the intended Parisian boulevard. *J. H. Taylforth collection/DRH*

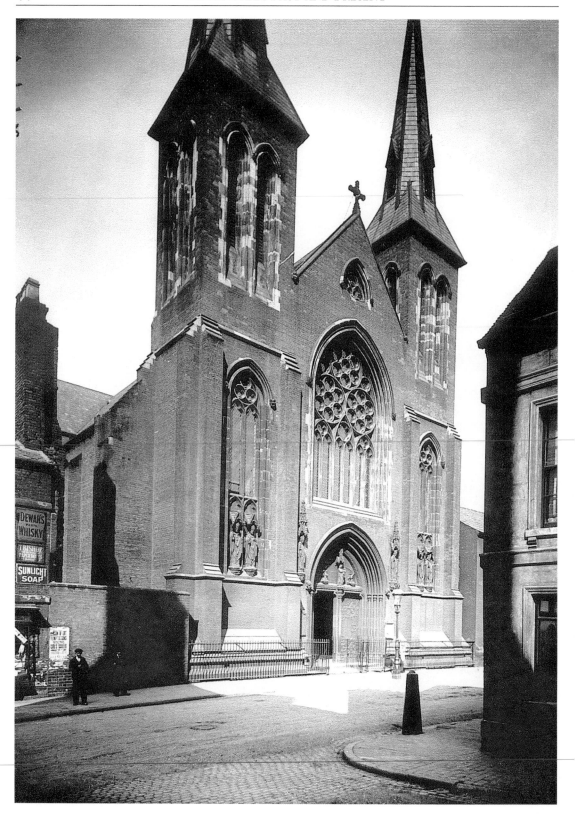

ST CHAD'S ROMAN CATHOLIC CATHEDRAL was built just to the north-east of Snow Hill and occupied a corner site, with its western towers facing Bath Street, while the Bishop's House and the associated school were round the corner in Shadwell Street. Built to the design of Augustus Welby Northmore Pugin (1812-52), Bishop Walsh laid the foundation stone on 29 October 1839. It was one of Pugin's earlier architectural commissions, although he had assisted Sir Charles Barry with the Neo-Tudor decorative detail of Westminster New Palace, better known as the Houses of Parliament, in 1834. Pugin was an avid researcher of medieval cathedral design, but because of his extremely intense nature his expertise eventually drove him to a nervous breakdown and early death. St Chad's was the first purpose-built Cathedral to be constructed since Sir Christopher Wren's St Paul's. More controversially, it was the first brick-built Cathedral to be constructed in this country, although that had not been the original intention. The building of St Chad's was sponsored by the Earl of Shrewsbury, a devout Roman Catholic, almost to the point of bankruptcy. It was his plan that the new structure would be built of stone, but having allocated his money to the interior, also designed by Pugin, the actual fabric of the exterior had to be completed in brick when the Earl's finances became exhausted. Pugin's design was in the manner of a 14th-century German Baltic Cathedral, with twin towers. However, because of financial problems, the second tower was not completed until 1856, some 15 years after its twin. The first photograph, dating from circa 1902, demonstrates Pugin's intended French locational style: originally the church was surrounded by 18th-century buildings occupied by local gunsmiths (the area around Lower Loveday Street, Price Street and Shadwell Street was known as the 'Gun Quarter' and for many years was as well known as the Jewellery Quarter in nearby Hockley). Pugin's aim was to copy French Cathedrals such as Chartres, Rouen, Rheims and Amiens that seem to 'emerge' as a splendid vision soaring from the surrounding small side streets and everyday buildings. However, by the time of the photograph many of the surrounding workshops and houses had been demolished, so Pugin's original idea was lost within 60 years of its inception. However, the buildings that remain near the west end still manage to capture the way in which Pugin had originally envisaged his masterpiece.

Pugin's idea of the 'rearing Cathedral' arising from the surrounding artisans' streets and dwellings is well illustrated by the second view of the west end of St Chad's in Bath Street in 1930. The Cathedral was built on a most awkward site, screwed into the side of Snow Hill, with Bath Street being the only fairly level street, though still hilly, among those surrounding the church. On the far side of the entrance are some of the late Georgian buildings, while on the corner of Shadwell Street are a group of early 19th-century buildings from which the Cathedral seems to emerge like a gigantic ship's prow. The run-down Walker's File and Tool Warehouse occupies the Shadwell Street corner, and its imminent demolition will expose St Chad's for the first time, but will also destroy Pugin's original plan for its location. Parked in Shadwell Street is a Sunbeam fabric-saloon, registered in Birmingham as OF 6037 during the first weeks of 1930. *Both Birmingham Archdiocesan Archives, reproduced by kind permission of His Grace the Archbishop of Birmingham*

The same view in 1955 shows the site after the demolition of Walker's premises, revealing for the first time the magnificent south-western aspect of St Chad's Cathedral. It also shows how Pugin's design had to cope with the awkward site with which he was faced. The Germanic style of the twin west towers, soaring into the heavens over Birmingham, is an extremely interesting architectural feature in the churches around Birmingham's city centre and, together with the small chapel on the Shadwell Street corner, can for the first time be appreciated. The short transepts make the exterior look somewhat truncated, as from this vantage point the traditional cruciform shape of the Cathedral is rather lost.

Viewed from the John F. Kennedy Memorial Gardens in St Chad's Circus in 2001, the Roman Catholic Cathedral still stands out impressively, although ironically this is not what Pugin had intended. Except for a small enclave, most of the buildings in the old 'Gun Quarter' have long since been demolished, leaving the Cathedral beautifully exposed and even more impressive for its modern-day isolation, bounded as it is on two sides by the Inner Ring Road scheme of the 1960s. *Birmingham Archdiocesan Archives, reproduced by kind permission of His Grace the Archbishop of Birmingham/DRH*

ENTERTAINMENTS

The entertainments offered in Birmingham over the years have ranged from local medieval markets with associated fairs and simple amusements and strolling entertainers to bare-knuckle boxing, cock-fighting and bear- and bull-baiting; the latter was a legal requirement in the 16th century, and a local bye-law obliged butchers to bait all bulls before the unfortunate animal was slaughtered as it was thought to tenderise the meat! Therefore out of necessity came a form of sport. Birmingham traditionally seemed to lack the cultural delights of live theatre. Being more involved in hard work and hard toil, in the days following the Industrial Revolution relaxation usually involved an inn or an ale-house.

The main problems with any entertainment in Birmingham were geographical and religious. The Tudor market town of Birmingham was, as Camden described it, 'swarming with people', yet had a population of barely 10,000, clustered around The Shambles, the Parish Church of St Martin, High Street and New Street. By 1731, on the strength of its market, geographical centrality and smithy industries, Birmingham's population had grown to 23,000, yet Georgian Birmingham still covered a surprisingly small area, the population still being concentrated within a half-mile radius of the Bull Ring. Despite the enormous increase in the population over the next century to 170,000, the town centre remained the same size and the first suburban areas grew basically to house the ever-increasing population. Throughout the Victorian period more and more theatres and music halls were concentrated in this geographically small town centre.

In 1740 the first theatre in Birmingham was opened in Moor Street. The landlords of the aforementioned ale-houses provided entertainment for men in much the same way as a visiting singer, small band or pop group might do in a present-day public house. Any larger places of entertainment were in the centre of the town, and the Theatre Royal in New Street, opened in 1774, was an important early example. It was at about this time that the strong Nonconformist opinion in the town began to become influential. They considered theatres immoral and opposed the construction of such places of entertainment. Although the growth of ale-houses with theatrical stages continued, eventually the typical Victorian music hall grew up, but the puritanical views of the Quakers and Unitarians blighted Birmingham's reputation as a place of entertainment for more than a century. Whereas Britain was at the centre of the 'Swinging Sixties', Birmingham's population largely missed it due to puritanical licensing laws for hostelries, theatres and cinemas. Even as late as the 1960s any act coming to perform in the city's theatres still had to submit its script to the Corporation's Watch Committee.

It was a Birmingham man, Alexander Parkes, an industrial chemist, who in 1862 invented a material he called 'Parkesine', which was later to form the basis of the roll film used in the photographic and cinematic industries. His invention was later renamed celluloid, and enabled projected moving pictures to be developed in France by Etienne Mary and the Lumière Brothers using the very same celluloid. The first film to be shown in the city was projected at the Birmingham & Midland Institute in Paradise Street in 1897; appropriately enough, in view of the city's bull-baiting history, it was of a bull-fight. The passing of the Cinematograph Act of 1909 opened the floodgates for the growth of cinemas, but it was not just the city centre that gained such places of entertainment. In all about 144 cinemas have been licensed in the city, yet unlike the theatres, which were concentrated in the city centre, only 14 cinemas were in the central area.

By the 1870s the small workshops in Birmingham that nurtured the characteristic artisan culture were being replaced by new, larger factories, and the ale-houses, the original places of entertainment, were losing out to the new, larger musical halls. As a result there was a surge in public house construction by speculative brewers and publicans who had a sharp eye for gimmicks to keep their newly found customers from succumbing to the Temperance movement. By the end of the Victorian period there was a pub or gin-house on nearly every suburban corner, and the town centre could boast more than 70 public houses and bars. However, nightlife in Birmingham was distinctly lacking, and when compared to London or even other provincial cities such as Manchester or Liverpool, Birmingham's famous all-night bus services were used mainly by factory workers changing late shifts rather than returning early morning revellers. By the early 1970s a few city centre clubs, such as the Rum Runner and the Opposite Lock Club, were beginning to attract the younger folk of Birmingham, and suddenly the old-fashioned pub was having to look for a new clientele. Leisure industries increased in importance as manufacturing industry in the city began to decline in the early 1980s, resulting in Birmingham City Council beginning to accept that leisure,

conference and tourist facilities were a way of putting the city on the cultural map of Britain. Gone at last was the stifling Quaker influence that had made the city look closed after 11.00pm. This change was the catalyst for plans to extend the city centre from within the confines of the Inner Ring Road, which was the area of mid-Georgian Birmingham, along Broad Street to Five Ways. In this was created the International Convention Centre, Centenary Square and Brindleyplace as well as revitalising, with award-winning schemes, the Gas Street canalside area.

This chapter examines the changes in the 'entertainment' industry in the city centre, concentrating on the theatres, cinemas and public houses, and gives an impression of the changes that have taken place over the last 100 or so years.

Perhaps Birmingham's most famous place of entertainment was the **THEATRE ROYAL** in New Street. Only pre-dated by the Moor Street Theatre of 1740 and The Theatre in King Street of 1751, it opened on 20 June 1774 as The New Theatre, presumably replacing the previous purpose-built premises in King Street. It changed its name in 1807 to the Theatre Royal, a date in its history that fell between two catastrophic fires, the first in 1792 and the second in 1820. The building that is best remembered is the 2,200-seat theatre opened on 16 December 1904. These new premises cost the huge amount, even for the early years of this century, of £30,000. The Theatre Royal became synonymous with musicals, variety shows and, perhaps most famously, its Christmas pantomime. During the Second World War variety acts such as The Crazy Gang, Tommy Trinder and Gracie Fields all appeared here. The 1954 pantomime was *Puss in Boots* with Jimmy Jewell and Ben Warriss, while in the following year it was *Old King Cole* starring Vic Oliver, with his one-line 'patter' gags and appalling violin playing! However, this turned out to be the last Christmas season at the Theatre Royal. The fading grandeur of red velour and golden-painted balconies and boxes was in need of restoration, but the refurbishment was never to happen – the lease was up! The final performance took place on Saturday 15 December 1956, with a production of *The Fol-de-Rols*, with the late Leslie Crowther in the cast, after which the curtain came down on the poor old Theatre Royal. It was an extremely sad loss. By the early months of the following year, as seen here, the scaffolding was up and demolition was well under way. If one walked down Ethel Street, the auditorium, for so long a place of entertainment and pleasure, was open to the skies as quite quickly the theatre was destroyed.

The Piccadilly Arcade next door to the doomed Theatre Royal is a strange survivor from another form of entertainment and is one of Birmingham's more interesting shopping arcades. It was opened on 20 October 1910 as The Picture House cinema, whose claim to fame was that it had a system for synchronised musical sound, although the 'Animataphone' method appears to have used 78rpm gramophone records played

in conjunction with the silent film performance. While the Picture House was not Birmingham's first cinema, it was one of only about five Edwardian picture houses in the city centre. It closed on 5 June 1926 and was converted into the Piccadilly Arcade (see Volume 1), although the facade of the cinema's upper storeys can be identified in the large arched frontage.

Further up New Street, just beyond Ethel Street, can just be made out the canopy of the Forum Cinema. This was originally the Masonic Hall, which had shown films by the Lumière Brothers as early as 1897. Variously named the Theatre de Luxe and the Regent, it was acquired by the ABC chain and re-opened on 1 November 1930; as the ABC it closed on 9 April 1983 after showing the Steven Spielberg film *ET*, and was the last place of entertainment in the top half of New Street, leaving the old Paramount, latterly the Odeon, at the High Street end to show films and stage live pop concerts. Beyond the cinema at the top end of New Street is the Town Hall and Victoria Square.

The 1990s pedestrianisation of New Street left a short section between Temple Street and Bennetts Hill available for limited vehicular access, and it is in this section of New Street that the fine Edwardian frontage of the Piccadilly Arcade has somehow survived, despite its dramatic change of function. The Theatre Royal site was redeveloped with the Woolworth Building, designed by Cotton, Ballard and Blow and built between 1961 and 1964. It was in many ways a strange-looking building, especially when viewed from any other elevation than that of New Street, rising in a series of blocks that gave the impression of a top-heavy 1920s passenger liner. Woolworth's 'new prestigious' shop in Broad Street had been abandoned in 1940 when only half completed, eventually becoming Bush House, the main offices of the Corporation Housing Departments. By the early 1960s their old Bull Ring premises in Spiceal Street was about to be demolished, so their shop at 61-65 New Street, next to Lyons Corner House, was replaced by the construction of this new multi-level shop on the Theatre Royal site. Their new Bull Ring Centre shop would not be ready for a few years.

Eventually, in the 1980s, Woolworth closed the New Street shop and after its sale the building was greatly enlarged with the addition of the glass and steel tower that can be seen at the Ethel Street end of the building in the 1999 view. The economic pressure that had driven the Theatre Royal out of New Street was also responsible for the demise of Woolworth as a city centre store, and today the building is occupied by sandwich bars, restaurants and office equipment shops. Through the trees can be seen the old ABC Forum Cinema, while the columns of the distant Town Hall, empty and awaiting renovation, stand overlooking the distant renovated Victoria Square. *J. Moss/DRH*

At the junction of Smallbrook Street and Hurst Street was a curious-looking public house, a single-storey building with what appeared to be a square block on the flat roof with a decorative hole in the side facing Hurst Street. Seen here in January 1952, it was called the Empire Vaults, and this name was a clue to its original use – the building was the remnants of the old **EMPIRE THEATRE**, which, rather co-incidentally, had been built on the site of the White Swan public house. The theatre opened on 7 May 1894, called the New Empire Palace of Varieties, which rather epitomised the type of entertainment that could be enjoyed. For most of its life it was part of the Moss Empires chain, which perhaps most famously included the 'graveyard of English comedians', the Glasgow Empire. The ground floor became the Empire Vaults, displaying the famous red triangular Bass sign on either side of the entrance. This was all that was left of the theatre when it was destroyed in an air-raid in October 1940. Although the lights are still on inside the pub, the building was demolished later the same year. Almost certainly the Empire Theatre would not have survived for very long into the post-war period anyway, as many variety theatres closed with the onslaught of television.

However, despite its fairly short life the theatre had one claim to fame. In November 1926 a show opened that would launch the 'top-of-the-bill' debut of probably the greatest comedian of British variety, still revered today. The show was called *Piccadilly* and its female lead was Florence Desmond, who

was only 21 years old and would later become a star herself, being best known for her impersonations and dancing. Top of the bill, however, was one Thomas Harry Sargent, born in Brighton on 21 November 1894 and who died on 8 May 1963. On Sargent's death, Arthur Askey said of him, 'He was the finest front-cloth comic I ever saw.' Charlie Chester, whose early career was often regarded as a poor parody, stated that 'he was the greatest stand-up comic who ever lived'. Eric Morecambe described him as 'the comic all comedians went to see', while his contemporary, Sandy Powell, saw him as 'the finest gag-merchant'. Even his arch-enemy, Tommy Trinder, said that 'he was a terrific performer'. Possibly the most glowing tribute was paid by Harry Worth, who commented that 'he was the best patter comic of them all; as an artist I have never seen his equal!' Who was he?

'Well, 'ave yer got it, lady? There'll never be another! Now there's a funny thing, I went home the other day...' He was the performer who by the middle of the 1930s was earning £1,000 a week, and who got his first top-of-the-bill slot in Birmingham. Later he was to vow that he would never play in a theatre in the city ever again after the Watch Committee fined him his week's wages for not sticking to the script. He was the great Max Miller, the immortal 'Cheeky Chappie'.

In the distance is the long-since-demolished tower of the Birmingham Hippodrome. This was opened on 9 October 1892 as the 'Tower of Varieties and Circus', a far cry from its

productions today. In theatrical terms, it has 'gone legit', being the home of the Birmingham Royal Ballet and Welsh National Opera. Today, the Hippodrome is also the home of Birmingham's premier Christmas pantomime, a lovely throwback to the wonderful age of variety that at one time thrived at numerous venues in Birmingham, including of course the Hippodrome itself.

Waiting for the traffic lights to change outside the Empire Vaults is a Coventry-registered Triumph Renown TDB. This is being followed by a Rolls-Royce 20/25 of about 1934 vintage and an Austin A70 Hampshire. Parked beneath the advertising hoarding for Mitchells & Butlers Export beer is an immediate pre-war Wolseley Series III six-cylinder saloon. Disappearing down Hurst Street and about to pass the Birmingham Hippodrome is a 1949 Daimler CVD6 bus belonging to the Corporation, working on the 48 route towards Balsall Heath. The remnants of the trolleybus overhead are still in place, the Coventry Road services that terminated in Station Street having only been abandoned at the end of the previous June, while the tramway infrastructure was by now only being used by the Cotteridge, Rednal and Rubery tramcars if they had to go to the main repair works in Kyotts Lake Road in Sparkbrook.

In the 'present' photograph, one of the two pairs of raked columns supporting the Ringway Centre as it vaults across Hurst Street is approximately at the site of the old Empire Vaults public house. Through the bridge is Hurst Street, and on the corner of Thorp Street is one of the few Victorian survivals between the Hippodrome, just visible to the right of the pair of distant trees, and the Smallbrook Queensway junction. In December 2002 enough money had been raised to restore these buildings to their original 'glory', as the sole surviving 'back-to-back' housing blocks anywhere in Birmingham. The demolition of this part of Smallbrook Street did not begin until early in 1957; the Ringway Centre buildings were designed by James A. Roberts in that year and were completed by 1962. This section of Birmingham's Inner Ring Road was the only part of the 2.25 miles of road to be built without the sole purpose of being a city centre by-pass; it included an impressive curve of shops, a hotel and offices on both sides of Smallbrook Queensway.

Hill Street subway, opposite Hurst Street, opened on 8 April 1959 and was the first of 52 pedestrian subways on the Inner Ring Road. It has since been closed and the Queensway lowered to accommodate surface-level pedestrian crossings. It is an indictment of the original concept to separate traffic from pedestrians that this, the first subway in the country, which was the only method by which pedestrians could cross the road, was replaced in the 1990s by a more 'people-friendly' street-level crossing. This was so successful that pedestrian subways elsewhere in the city centre were similarly removed. *Birmingham City Engineer & Surveyor's Dept/DRH*

The tram tracks in **JOHN BRIGHT STREET** saw their last tram some eight months earlier, as people wait at the 61, 62 and 63 replacement bus stops in February 1953. The road works and the road-roller are in connection with the lifting of the redundant tram tracks. In the distance a 1950-built Park Royal-bodied Leyland 'Titan' PD2/1 bus is about to cross the Smallbrook Street-Horsefair junction as it manoeuvres into Holloway Head, working its way via Five Ways to the 95 route terminus in Ladywood. Beyond the bus is the tower of St Catherine of Siena Roman Catholic Church, which was pulled down in the early 1960s and replaced by a circular-plan domed church in 1964. All the buildings on the right were demolished in the mid-1960s as part of the preparations for the construction of Suffolk Street Queensway. The attractive bay-windowed building on the corner of Station Street accommodated Ascott Dental Surgeries on the corner, J. Frank Brockliss, who supplied cinematography apparatus –projectors, bulbs and filters – and

Albert Whitehurst Gibson, who was an estate agent. The derelict buildings on Suffolk Street, behind the advertising hoardings that mask what as children we used to call a 'bomb-building site', had included a shop furniture supplier and a radio dealer, but they wouldn't be in those premises for much longer. The three vehicles parked alongside the hoardings are a Hillman Minx Phase I, an Austin A40 van and a Vauxhall Velox LIP; the van is virtually new while the two cars both date from about 1948.

When the Alexandra Theatre opened on 27 May 1901 as The Lyceum, its main entrance was in John Bright Street. A little over 18 months later it was renamed after the newly crowned Queen. The 'Alex', as it was known in Birmingham, was for many years run by the Salberg family, Leon from 1911 until his death 'in harness' in 1938, then his son, Derek, until his retirement in 1977. Under the latter's direction the theatre became known for attracting well-known plays and musicals and for its Christmas pantomime season. The theatre was expanded in 1968 when the impending redevelopment in John Bright Street would leave its main entrance in a backwater location, instead of the important routeway out of the city in which it had been built. The result was that a new entrance and lobby were constructed on Suffolk Street Queensway on the corner of Severn Street, linked to the main auditorium by the bridge over John Bright Street. Not long after this the theatre fell on very hard times and it was 'touch and go' as to whether it would survive, but fortunately with local government help and a lot of independent fund-raising, the Alex not only survived but today is a thriving place of thespian entertainment. The old line of John Bright Street was cut by the construction of Smallbrook Queensway and only the short section of Station Street, with the Victoria public house, opened in 1884, remaining. The distant NCP car park in the 1999 photograph is about where the people were waiting for their bus in 1953. Towering over the theatre block is one of the two 'Sentinel' 32-storey blocks of flats that stand on either side of Holloway Head, into which, nearly 50 years before, the Leyland bus working to Ladywood was about to turn. *Birmingham City Engineer & Surveyor's Dept/DRH*

Below At first sight, this looks like a view taken before the Second World War. There is a mid-1930s Morris Eight tourer on the right and the two pre-war Birmingham City Transport Daimler COG5 double-deckers in Broad Street. There are, however, certain clues that show that this scene was taken in about 1947. First, the two buses have khaki-painted roofs, a feature that was introduced in the early days of the war, when the all-over cream roof was replaced in an attempt to camouflage the buses in the event of an air-raid. Second, the bus stop is of a type that dates from after the war. However, the most telling clue involves the building on the extreme right. This is the **PRINCE OF WALES THEATRE**, which has its sign outside and looks ready for its next performance, but closer examination reveals that the entrance is boarded up and most of the glass canopy is missing, which is not altogether surprising as the auditorium was destroyed on 9 April 1941 in an air-raid.

The Prince of Wales opened as long ago as 3 September 1856 as The Birmingham Music Hall, and by 1865 had become The Prince of Wales. After the war its gutted interior was incorporated into the adjacent Bingley Hall, leaving the facade

on Broad Street as a gaunt reminder of its thespian past until its demolition in 1987. Beyond King Edward's Place is the elegant early 19th-century Crown public house, which was used from 1875 by William Butler to brew his own beer. A large tower brewery was built behind the pub, and eventually about 5,000 barrels a week were produced at the Broad Street premises. Production ceased in 1898 when the amalgamation with Henry Mitchell's Crown Brewery took place and all production was moved to his Cape Hill premises in Smethwick. The large church with the Gothic spire is the Unitarians' Church of the Messiah, which was built with funds from the sale to the Roman Catholics of their New Meeting House premises off Moor Street (see pages 38-41). The church was completed in 1862 to the design of J. J. Bateman and its size and location reflected the importance of the Unitarian movement in the city, which counted the Nettlefold and Chamberlain families as members. The church was cunningly constructed on arches beneath which was the Birmingham Canal. It was demolished in April 1978. Beyond is the two-storey building called the Brasshouse, on the corner of Brasshouse Passage, which at this time was occupied by the City Weights & Measures Department.

The rebuilt Broad Street from Gas Street out of the city towards Five Ways has managed to retain many of its original buildings, and it is just possible to imagine the Morris Eight tourer travelling along the Broad Street of today. The £200 million-plus construction of the International Convention Centre on the site of Bingley Hall and the old Prince of Wales Theatre necessitated the demolition of several listed buildings in Alfred Place and St Peter's Place (see Volume 1), but the impact of the ICC on Broad Street was profound. New hotels, such as the five-star Hyatt Regency and the Novotel further up Broad Street on the site of Bush House, the old Corporation Housing Department headquarters, as well as places of entertainment changed a rather drab road into one of the new 'bright light' areas of the city. It also meant that a number of the older buildings were either renovated or totally rebuilt for another purpose. The Crown Hotel, although losing its old disused brewery buildings, was extensively renovated. The gap between it and the Brasshouse building, itself converted to a pub-cum-restaurant, is where the old Church of the Messiah straddled the Birmingham Canal on its way to the hidden basin off Gas Street. Access to the canal towpath and the huge Brindleyplace commercial development has changed this section of Broad Street, while the planting of trees coupled with the widening of the pavements has been a welcome attempt to improve the local environment. The tower of a further converted building, the classically styled Presbyterian Second Church of Christ Scientist, built unusually in Staffordshire blue brick in 1849, has also survived in a non-ecclesiastical form. The buildings on the left were derelict for a number of years but were retained because of their early 20th-century Art Nouveau interest and are now largely converted to bars. *Commercial postcard/DRH*

Below The **BIRMINGHAM REPERTORY THEATRE** in Centenary Square was originally in Station Street and opened on 15 February 1913 with a production of Shakespeare's *Twelfth Night*. The theatre became world famous under the direction of Sir Barry Jackson, with some of the giants of the English stage, such as Laurence Olivier, Felix Aylmer, John Gielgud, Ralph Richardson, Edith Evans and Peggy Ashcroft, having seasons of 'rep' in Station Street. By 1931 the theatre's General Manager was Emile Littler, who was later to become one of the country's major theatrical impresarios. By the late 1960s, however, it was becoming obvious that the theatre's seating capacity of 450 was inadequate, and the necessity for a new, larger theatre became a reality when the City Council gave £640,000 towards the total cost of £1 million. The new theatre's foundation stone was laid by the then Chairman of the Arts Council, the Rt Hon Jennie Lee MP, on 25 October 1969, and the theatre was opened on 20 October 1971 by HRH Princess Margaret. With 901 seats, it was a huge improvement on the old Station Street premises, which is still open as the 'Old Rep'. Adjacent to the main auditorium of the new theatre is the Studio Theatre, where normally small-scale productions of contemporary works are performed. The Studio has a seating capacity of 120.

The Broad Street theatre was built with a very open plan, and its front elevation, looking out originally on to a small paved area overlooking Broad Street, was rather more glass than concrete. Immediately behind the glass front are numerous bars and refreshment areas as well as an excellent restaurant, while running through the length of the theatre behind these is a spacious foyer. It was one of the first places in Birmingham where, weather permitting, one could sit outside on the 'boardwalk' to enjoy a coffee or something stronger. It was another 20 years before the rest of Broad Street caught up with 'The Rep'. New conference rooms have been built on the Baskerville House side of the theatre on the right, but the greatest changes have occurred in the area surrounding the theatre, with the building of the International Convention Centre, whose entrance canopy is on the left, and Tess Jaray's splendid brickwork in Centenary Square. *DRH*

Left Many of the buildings in **EASY ROW** facing Broad Street dated from the mid-1760s and in their time were rather attractive Georgian town houses; later converted to offices, even in the late 1940s they looked in quite good condition. They are the heavily porticoed three-storied buildings on the extreme left of this circa 1947 view. In front of them is the traffic island at the bottom of Broad Street, opposite the Hall of Memory. The island is being negotiated by one of the four 8-feet-wide Daimler COG6 double-deckers built for Johannesburg Municipal Transport in South Africa, but which were diverted to Birmingham Corporation because enemy U-boat activity in the Atlantic in 1941 prevented their delivery. The bus is working on the 9 service to Quinton, which was the only route in the early post-war period on which these extra-wide buses were allowed to operate. It is passing the huge West End Chambers Building, which was built adjacent to the site of the Birmingham Canal Navigation offices just before the First World War; standing on the corner of Easy Row and Broad Street, it was at this time the main city office of the Britannic Assurance Company. The building was demolished in the early 1960s and today is the site of Alpha Tower.

The section from Paradise Street to Edmund Street in the centre of the view was much narrower than the rest of the street, seemingly hemmed in by taller buildings, which tended to give the 50 or so yards of this part of Easy Row a somewhat gloomy appearance. It also had running through it traffic converging from both Suffolk Street, which is the road running up the steep hill immediately behind the Corporation bus, and Paradise Street, from which the two cars behind the bus have just emerged. It was in this narrow part of Easy Row that the famous Woodman public house stood, which can just be seen as the building on the left with the single Dutch-gable roof embellishment.

The view from Broad Street in 1999 towards the city centre shows an array of modern buildings that form a 'wall' of development on the line of the old Easy Row. On the left is the Central Reference Library, opened in 1973. Next to it is the equally controversial black-glassed frontage of the Copthorne Hotel, which opened its doors on 1 April 1987. The white building with the small windows some way behind the Travel West Midlands double-deck MCW Metrobus Mk II is the School of Music. This had been completed at the same time as the library, but for many years the whole complex was left unfinished, with a never-used bus station beneath it. It is on about this site that the long-lamented Woodman public house stood. Through the complex, linking the School of Music to the Central Library, is a small shopping mall called Fletcher's Walk, named in honour of one of The Woodman's most famous landlords. It is a nice touch, but in some ways it is a sad reminder of what was

probably the finest example of a Victorian hostelry in the city centre. Ironically, the latest proposals are that this site, including the Central Reference Library, will be closed in about 2005 when the library will be transferred to the new Millennium Point development in Digbeth. *Commercial postcard/DRH*

Below **THE WOODMAN** in Easy Row was a three-storey building constructed in 1891 to the design of Henry Naden. It featured a large alcove at first-floor level, which had in it a statue of a woodman with his faithful dog and an axe over his shoulder. Naden's design for the upper storeys had a faintly Flemish Renaissance look about it, but it was at ground level that he was able to give vent to the best of his flamboyant vagaries. Just visible in this circa 1895 photograph are the oriel windows and large carved wooden frieze, and the main door that enticed the customer to sample the delights within (see overleaf). When it was built, some of the Corporation's committees met in the first-floor function room as this was a suitable overflow, in every sense of the word, from the already overused Council House committee rooms. The Woodman had been built on the site of some of the worst slum properties in the city and was always intended to be one of the most prestigious hostelries in Birmingham. As a result, it became one of the city's most famous public houses, not just because of its popularity with Council staff, University students and students from the School of Art in Margaret Street, but because of its interior fixtures and fittings. *Author's collection*

The Public Bar of **THE WOODMAN**, seen in the first photograph, was tiled throughout, and among the majolica-glazed tiles were a series of tiled pictures depicting scenes around 18th-century Birmingham. The nearest one on the right shows the famous Digbeth tripe house, while other scenes included views over the Bull Ring market towards St Martin's Church and the way Hill Street looked immediately after the Town Hall had been built. With its leather-covered benches, the snob screens and the heavily carved woodwork on the front of the bar counter, the pub had some of the finest examples of late-Victorian public house fixtures and fittings in the city. They were obviously worth saving for posterity, but The Woodman closed in December 1964 and was, with criminal lack of thought, demolished shortly afterwards.

The long Smoke Room, seen in the other two photographs, was even more magnificent. The selection of filled bread rolls in the cabinet, the two wooden hand-pumps and the gilded cash register behind the elaborately carved wooden corner bar appear ready to entice any prospective customer to sit down and enjoy the unaltered surroundings of this lovely Victorian room. The Smoke Room was opened a year after the rest of the pub and was a remarkable survivor as it retained all its original 19th-century fixtures and fittings to the end. The lower photograph shows the elaborate fireplace with its multi-pillared canopied area in front. Had The Woodman survived for a few more years, it might well have been saved or incorporated into the Paradise Circus redevelopment in much the same way as The Crown in Broad Street. Today there are a few suburban public houses that have retained their tiling and their character, including the Bartons Arms in Newtown, Aston, and the Hare & Hounds in Kings Heath. *All MRK Enterprises collection*

The **WEST END CINEMA** opened on 9 March 1925, and as early as August 1929 had begun to show sound films. It was famous for its electric organ, a 2/8 Wurlitzer that was first played by Charles Willis in 1926 and was frequently played by such well-known theatre organists of the day as Reginald Dixon, Sandy MacPherson and Reginald Fforte. The cinema was due to close in April 1965 as part of the redevelopment necessary for the Inner Ring Road scheme, and all the buildings in Suffolk Street towards Broad Street had been demolished by the previous year. This corner site at the junction with Broad Street was earmarked for use by the then franchised local commercial Associated Television company (ATV), whose previous premises in Aston Road, in the old Astoria Cinema, was known as the Alpha Television Studios; when the new building was finally approved, therefore, the imposing 30-storey 'skyscraper' was given the name Alpha Tower. Meanwhile, the West End Cinema was given a reprieve and continued as such until 18 March 1967, when it showed its last film, *The Return of the Seven* starring Yul Brynner. Not long after the first 'past' photograph was taken, in July 1966, from the corner of Paradise Street, from where the Morris Minor Traveller is emerging, the West End showed the documentary of England's victory in the World Cup. This was a revelation as it was in colour; the BBC Television coverage, including Kenneth Wolstenholme's famous remark 'They think it's all over … it is now!' as Geoff Hurst scored his hat-trick goal in extra time, was in glorious black and white. The showing of this documentary was therefore something of an Indian summer coup for the old West End.

The second view is looking up Suffolk Street towards the West End in early 1967, and on the corner of Allport Street, behind the Vauxhall Victor FB, are the former Midland Railway Central Goods Offices (although the entablature on the Suffolk Street side refers to it as the Central Goods 'Station'). The offices served the Central goods yard, which was to the left of where the Corporation bus is standing. This had been opened in 1887 as the Worcester Wharf Goods Depot and had relieved the increasingly congested Lawley Street goods sheds and sidings. It remained an important railway goods yard for Birmingham for quite a few more years, whereas the Allport Street offices were demolished in about 1967 as part of the land clearances required for the completion of the Inner Ring Road scheme. Allport Street was the terminus of the 95 bus service to Ladywood. This had replaced the 33 tram route on 30 August 1947, which had formerly terminated in Navigation Street in company with the trams that ran along Bristol Road and to Cotteridge. On leaving Allport Street, the bus would turn right into Holliday Street alongside the West End cinema and turn into Suffolk Street where the GPO Morris LD-type van is standing. The bus is 2224 (JOJ 224), a Leyland 'Titan' PD2/1, with a Park Royal body, which spent most of its working life at Rosebery Street garage working on the Dudley Road services. These buses were ordered as tram replacement vehicles and had normal Southall-style bodies that were embellished to Birmingham standard. Most of them ran for about 18 years and one of the class, 2222 (JOJ 222), has been preserved at the Aston Manor Transport Museum.

The demolition of the buildings between the West End Cinema and Broad Street allow Baskerville House to be seen at the top of Suffolk Street. This building would have become part of the much larger Civic Centre planned in the mid-1930s for Broad Street, but impressive though it is, it was destined to be the only part of the scheme to be completed, as the rest of the plan was never implemented after the Second World War. Baskerville House is known by council staff as 'The Kremlin', not necessarily because of any political leanings by the local council, but because the building's architectural style has certain Moscovite overtones!

Dominating the corner of Suffolk Street Queensway and Broad Street in 2000 is the Alpha Tower complex and Central Square. ATV required prestigious television studios in the centre of Birmingham and the then Conservative-led Birmingham Council was persuaded to grant the company a 125-year lease on the site. Alpha Tower was begun in 1970 and was recently granted special status as a possible listed building to celebrate its 30th birthday. Beneath the footbridge straddling Holliday Street is the 320-room Holiday Inn, which was built at the same time. The semi-circular ramp of the footbridge stands approximately on the site of the West End Cinema. The only point of reference between the two views is the distant and now empty Baskerville House, which now stands on the edge of Centenary Square awaiting conversion into a hotel. Just visible to the left of the road sign is the Hall of Memory's domed roof. This had been built in 1924 as a memorial to Birmingham's dead servicemen of the First World War. *MRK Enterprises Collection (2)/DRH*

THE INNER RING ROAD

The idea of building an 'inner ring' road around the city centre was first suggested in 1917 during Neville Chamberlain's three-year tenure as Lord Mayor. It had been realised that the congested city centre, with its narrow shopping streets, would require some relief from the ever-increasing traffic, but the early post-war restrictions were not a conducive economic climate for such a grand plan. By the late 1920s the situation was so bad that in 1930 a special Traffic Control Committee was set up to look at the problem of congestion. The results of its deliberations were implemented on 5 June 1933 when the famous one-way-street system was introduced. This scheme relieved the situation that had resulted in traffic taking half an hour to go from Victoria Square to Bull Street by way of New Street. It also resulted in Birmingham becoming the butt of the motoring press and music hall comedians as possessing a system of roads that, once inside, could become an impenetrable maze in which strangers to the city would be lost for ever, driving around looking for an escape route until they died of exhaustion!

In 1943 the Advisory (Traffic) Planning Panel reported to the City Council that the original plans for an Inner Ring Road should be revived. The plans suggested that traffic not going into the city centre should be diverted away from it, that shopping streets should not be wide traffic arteries, and that buses should be able to circulate within the city centre and should bring passengers into the heart of the city. Strangely, one of the precepts was that the scheme should encourage the spread of first-class shopping and commercial areas beyond the traditional 'loop'; unfortunately, once constructed the new road was to have exactly the opposite effect and was to become a concrete stranglehold around the city centre! The new road would be a dual-carriageway of at least 110 feet and, uniquely in this country, was to be designed primarily as a traffic road and not generally intended to have frontages for shops, offices or warehouses. There would be seven main junctions with the incoming arterial roads, which would be provided with large traffic islands. This was a very '1930s' concept and these roundabouts would become 'The Achilles' Heel' of the Inner Ring Road scheme.

The City Council approved the plans in July 1944, and by the end of the year it had received the necessary Parliamentary Bill, but unfortunately the scheme was held up for the next 12 years by the Ministry of Transport and a general lack of capital in 'cash-strapped' post-war Britain. Meanwhile, some 85 acres of land and over 1,200 buildings were compulsorily acquired in preparation. Eventually the Minister of Transport, the Rt Hon Harold Wilkinson MP, gave approval for the scheme on 18 January 1957. On 8 March he detonated a charge of gelignite at the ceremonial starting ceremony, which injured one of the 'gentlemen of the local press'. It was an inauspicious start!

The first section to be started was from the junction of Horsefair and Smallbrook Street to the junction with Worcester Street. These 400 yards cost £1.16 million and was to be the only section to be lined with offices and retail premises. The graceful curve of the Ringway Centre on the south side of Smallbrook Queensway (see page 51) was completed in 1961, not long after the first section was opened on 11 March 1960 by the man who launched the Premium Bond, the new Minister of Transport, Ernest Marples. It was the most successful section of the ringway as it included Ringway House, Norfolk House and the 14-storey Albany Hotel. This prestigious new road, with its red-coloured tarmac, was to remain isolated for two years while the next section through the Bull Ring to Carrs Lane was constructed. The link into the city from St Chad's Circus, along Snow Hill through Colmore Circus, Old Square to Lower Priory, was completed by 1964, while the elevated section across Masshouse Circus to Lancaster Place was completed soon after. The original plans were modified during construction by the replacement of the roundabouts with a two-level junction at Holloway Head and a three-level junction at Lancaster Place. This north-western section became the major route from the M5 at Lydiate Ash to the M6 at Gravelly Hill via the Aston Expressway (A38M), and the south-west of the city to the north-east, and included the half-mile-long tunnel between Suffolk Street and Great Charles Street.

The completed Inner Ring Road was opened for traffic on 4 January 1971, and officially opened by HM The Queen on 7 April. In an unintentional gaff in her opening speech, Her Majesty referred to the whole 2.25-mile-long 'Ringway' as 'The Queensway', so the whole road was renamed. With its 52 pedestrian subways, it was initially a great success, but even before its completion, its shortcomings were becoming apparent. Pedestrians disliked their subterranean crossing points, which were soon areas covered with graffiti, urine-stained and at night places that rapidly attracted criminal activity. It took nearly 20 years before a start was made to remedy the situation by the gradual elimination of the pedestrian subways, putting people first and relegating the cars to either the same level as pedestrians, as in Smallbrook Queensway at Hurst Street, or below the level of the pedestrians, as at the junction of Paradise Circus and Broad Street, reconstructed in 1989.

The road, however, had another more unfortunate consequence. It acted like a concrete collar around the city 'heartland' and strangled any new development beyond it, mainly because access was so difficult. The internationally acclaimed £8 million Bull Ring Shopping Centre, opened by HRH The Duke of Edinburgh on 29 May 1964, quickly became a 'white elephant' as it was on the 'wrong side of the Queensway' and had appalling pedestrian access. The wholesale and retail markets also suffered, and soon the Bull Ring, so long the focus for the Brummie, had been reduced to a concrete hole in the ground that soon made many people who worked and shopped in the area hanker after the 'good old days' of the recently demolished Market Hall. In St Chad's Queensway, the road had been ruthlessly driven through the 'Gun Quarter', which resulted in the loss of many eminently restorable Georgian properties. It was only the construction of Centenary Square and the International Convention Centre in the Broad Street Redevelopment Area, designated in 1987 and completed by 1991, that encouraged further redevelopment along Broad Street at Brindleyplace.

The rebuilding, again, of the Bull Ring began in 2000 with the elimination of 'the hole', while work began in 2001 to remove the elevated Masshouse Circus, which

has caused development blight in the Albert Street-Curzon Street-Bartholomew Street part of town ever since it was constructed. The increase in traffic using the western and northern tunnels, especially vehicles using the Inner Ring Road to gain access to the Aston Expressway, made the Queensway intolerable, especially during rush-hour periods, thus somewhat defeating the original purpose of the road. As a result, since 1991 cross-city traffic has been encouraged to use the newly completed Middle Ring Road. This downgrading of the Inner Ring Road has enabled schemes to take place on Smallbrook Queensway and Paradise Circus, partially enabling people to come out of their troglodyte existence and giving the ring road back to the pedestrian. The proposals for the Bull Ring will put vehicles beneath the new development and make the area effectively traffic-free, but easily accessible from the city centre, while the demolition of Masshouse Circus will allow better access to the new Millennium Point development on the recently renamed East Side, which lies behind Digbeth.

The Inner Ring Road was a hugely influential project, but it had as many disadvantages as advantages. The road was conceived in the first half of the last century when traffic was being perceived as a problem. It was begun in 1957 and completed 14 years later when 'King Car' ruled. Birmingham was called Car City at this time, not only because of its numerous volume car manufacturers, but also because of the sheer volume of traffic that passed through the area. As an aside, the congestion around the M6 and M5 motorways to the north of the city, which regularly has a knock-on effect on the Inner Ring Road via the A38(M) Aston Expressway and the Gravelly Hill interchange, is now so bad that the Birmingham Northern Relief Road, which will be Britain's first toll motorway, is under construction.

The third stage in the life-cycle of the Inner Ring Road, which will soon be approaching its 85th year since it was originally proposed, began in the 1990s. The first successful attempts to re-introduce people back to parts of the Queensway will continue into the first decade of the 21st century and will eliminate most of the pedestrian subways and improve access across the road from the city centre. For the first time in many years the economic blight and physical stranglehold of the Inner Ring Road will be broken.

Right **SMALLBROOK STREET** was the location of the first section of the Inner Ring Road; named after a Yardley-based family who took their name from a brook near their ancestral home, it linked the former turnpike roads to the south-west and west of the town with the market areas. Although it was obviously a road of some importance, Smallbrook Street was largely unused by Corporation bus services, being extensively used by Midland Red. In about 1935, Midland Red SOS IM4 – 'Improved Madam', 4-cylinder' (petrol-engined, of course) – with a 34-seat Short Brothers body of 1931, stands outside John Devoti's confectionery shop just beyond the Hurst Street junction, loading passengers for the 147 service to Alvechurch and Redditch. Despite their antiquated looks, these lightweight buses were considered to be very fast for their time, being the equal in performance terms, if not for looks, with the products of the major proprietary manufacturers. This example, HA 8201, would become numbered 1279 in 1944 and would survive in service until 1950. Behind the bus is the entrance to the Empire Theatre, which was destroyed in an air-raid on 24 October 1940 (see page 51). Smallbrook Street's buildings, including that of George Hull, drysalter, oil, varnish and paint manufacturer, on the far corner of Hurst Street, had the imposing look of buildings that belonged in the centre of Birmingham. Smallbrook Street was *that* important! *Warwickshire Local Studies Collection*

Below The demolition of properties on the line of the proposed Inner Ring Road did not officially begin until early in 1957. As leases expired, compulsory purchase orders were issued and the buildings were quickly pulled down. On 18 September 1956 George Hull's four-storey building on the corner of Smallbrook Street and Hurst Street is already doomed. It has only recently been closed down, and the company has moved to similar premises on the corner of Horsefair and Essex Street. Second-hand building materials saved from the interior of the building are being advertised for sale just before the demolishers, Birmingham Mid Demolition Co, begin serious action. The demolisher's

signs warn pedestrians of the impending removal of the property while they are negotiating the scaffolding that already encases the once elegant late-19th-century building. Also affected by the demolition are Mentor's shirt shop in Hurst Street and Proctor's tailors and Johnson's jewellery shops in Smallbrook Street. Behind the Austin Three-Way van, the older buildings in Smallbrook Street are also announcing their impending closure.

Travelling down Smallbrook Street towards the distant Edgbaston Street-Worcester Street junction is an early example of a vehicle with a reversed registration – 650 DMX is an Austin A50 registered by Middlesex CC – while in front of it is an Austin FX3 taxi. They are passing an early Bedford CA, which was the Ford Transit of its day. Near the Worcester Street junction is a BMMO D7 double-decker, which is continuing the Midland Red tradition of using Smallbrook Street as an access route to Horsefair and Bristol Street. The black-and-white-banded traffic lights are a remnant of wartime, when street lighting at night was sufficiently restricted that white edgings on vehicles and kerbs and white bands on trees and street furniture were essential to prevent collisions and accidents in the pitch darkness. On both corners of Hurst Street are pillars, which although not exactly horse-posts for tying-up equestrian-pulled vehicles, are redolent of that mode of transport. A long-forgotten piece of street furniture is to be seen on the extreme right: a red-painted fire alarm box that contains a telephone linked directly to the local fire station. This system pre-dated the emergency 999 calls that could be made from a telephone box. *Birmingham City Engineer & Surveyor's Dept*

The junction of Smallbrook Street with Horsefair on the right and the double junction with Suffolk Street and John Bright Street on the left at **HOLLOWAY HEAD** had been a major intersection since John Bright Street was constructed in 1881. By March 1947, bomb damage on the corner of Hurst Street, further down Smallbrook Street, had inadvertently started the process of breaking up the area. This in turn encouraged the first stages of the Inner Ring Road scheme to be started in this part of the city centre. The tram turning into Holloway Head from John Bright Street is car number 733, numerically the second vehicle of the 30 totally enclosed air-braked bogie trams built by the Brush

Electrical Engineering Co between September 1926 and March 1927. It is working on the 2½-mile-long 33 route that went to Ladywood by way of Five Ways before terminating in Icknield Port Road at its junction with Dudley Road. This was the second post-war tramway abandonment, going on 30 August 1947, which is when this photograph was taken. Although the war had ended over two years before, much of the street furniture still carries the previously mentioned white wartime blackout markings, such as on the tramway traction pole on the right next to the parked Morris Eight Series E. Just beyond it and to the right of the tram are the street bollards that mark the beginning of Smallbrook Street, where an Austin K-type lorry is parked outside the Scala Cinema.

Opened on 4 March 1914, the Scala had a seating capacity of 800 and was always regarded as one of the more luxurious of the city centre cinemas. Distinguished by its white stone facade and round-topped central bay, it was one of the first 'victims' of the start of the Inner Ring Road construction in 1957, finally closing its doors on 4 June 1960 after showing *Teenage Lovers* and *The Leech Woman*. The effects of wartime bombing are visible beyond the cinema as a gaunt, exposed gable-end; ten properties were destroyed here in 1940, and for the next 15 years the site was used by Hippodrome Motors as a second-hand car lot. Beyond the tall building is Hurst Street, where there is a wartime Corporation Bus travelling into the city centre. *D. R. Harvey collection*

The section of **SMALLBROOK QUEENSWAY** between Holloway Head and the Bull Ring was perhaps its most impressive. Standing on the line of the old Smallbrook Street, it cut a swathe through the Victorian shops and market area to the south of New Street Station. The curved six-storey buildings on the right were designed by James A. Roberts and were completed in 1961. The same architect designed the Albany Hotel on the opposite side of the dual carriageway, which dates from the following year. This 14-storey hotel was the first to be built in the city centre since the turn of the century and is now known as the Post House Hotel. Reclining in the traffic island at the bottom of Holloway Head is the bronze nude figure of Hebe, daughter of the Greek gods Zeus and Hera. She was the goddess of Youth and Spring and cup-bearer to Olympus. The statue was placed here to mark the position of the first ceremonial demolition in preparation for the Inner Ring Road scheme, which was begun near this site on 8 March 1957. Hebe lies gracefully not far from where the tram had turned into Holloway Head in 1947. *DRH*

The construction of the buildings along Smallbrook Ringway was well under way by 11 February 1959. Known as the Ringway Centre, the continuous development along the south side of the road was carried over **HURST STREET** on two pairs of raked columns (see also page 51). The uncompleted concrete skeleton shows that the apparently slender columns over the pedestrian underpass and the Hurst Street junction were not continued within the structure of the upper storeys. Throughout the construction of this showcase section of the Inner Ring Road scheme, the Hurst Street junction was kept open to all traffic, which was a tremendous achievement by Laing in view of the civil engineering involved in this part of the development, which would take nearly another two years to complete. On the right is the still fairly new wholesale distribution depot of newsagent W. H. Smith. On the opposite side of Hurst Street, on the corner of Thorp Street, is the Empire Commercial Hotel, its name a reminder of the old Empire Theatre that stood in Smallbrook Street about where the left-hand columns of the Ringway Centre stand. The cars are typical of the 1950s. That in the foreground is a Mercedes-Benz 190SL roadster, the only continental interloper among the British models. Parked behind is a Hillman

Minx Phase VII, the same model as the distant car negotiating the rise in the road over the still incomplete Smallbrook Ringway and its pedestrian underpass. Outside the Empire Commercial Hotel is a West Bromwich-registered Austin A55, while behind it is a two-tone Jaguar Mark VIIM.

Forty years later the Ringway Centre, by now the long-forgotten name of the building leaping over Hurst Street, has become a mature-looking structure. The design of the building, although very late-1950s in style, has stood the test of time better than some of its contemporaries, and it appears to have escaped proposals to demolish it. What has been altered is that the pedestrian subway, opened in April 1959 and the first in the country, was removed in the mid-1990s to allow pedestrians for the first time to walk in a much more pleasant environment at street level. From this aspect the disappearing Travel West Midlands Leyland 'Lynx' travelling across Smallbrook Queensway towards the city centre appears to be negotiating a road layout little altered since the Ringway was opened and the exhaust smoke from the Hillman Minx in the 1959 photograph drifted away. Careful examination reveals, however, that there are no cavernous openings adjacent to those

large inclined supporting pillars. The old Empire Commercial Hotel has for many years been an Indian restaurant, surviving both many changes in ownership and fires in the last 25 years, and now called the Maharaja. Occupying the former W. H. Smith warehouse is the China Palace conglomerate. On the far side of the Queensway and dwarfing everything else is the multi-storey office complex known as Centre City, built on the corner of Hinckley Street and Hill Street on what had originally been a site reserved for the Moss Empires Group to build a new theatre. What did reach fruition was the Physical Enhancement Strategy of 1987, which included plans to partly pedestrianise the Chinese Quarter around Ladywell Walk and part of Hurst Street, both behind the camera in this view; this included the area in front of the Birmingham Hippodrome, although the construction of the Arcadian Centre considerably enhanced the lower part of Hurst Street (see Volume 1). *Birmingham City Engineer & Surveyor's Dept/DRH*

The gentle curving profile of Ringway House has been almost completed along the frontage of Smallbrook Ringway (later **SMALLBROOK QUEENSWAY**) looking from the Hurst Street junction on 22 February 1960. What is apparent is that Laing, the contractor, is building the long retail and office block in a series of units so that while the section across Hurst Street is virtually finished, that at the Edgbaston Street end is still a skeleton with a huge swinging crane towering above it. The carriageway is only lacking its top surface, which when it was finally completed had red-coloured tar that had quite a novelty value. This 400-yard section of the road would be finally opened just 17 days later on 11 March 1960 by the Rt Hon Ernest Marples MP, the new Conservative Minister of Transport. Despite the imminence of the opening, there seems a distinct lack of urgency considering the amount of work obviously necessary prior to the official ribbon-cutting ceremony!

By 1999 Smallbrook Queensway had become a slightly down-at-heel shopping area catering for music, photographic and hi-fi enthusiasts and not, by and large, for the 'mainstream' shoppers for which it had been intended, who still went into the traditional 'city centre' shopping areas bounded by New Street and Corporation Street. The shops have always struggled to survive in a 'white elephant' that might have been a planner's dream but in reality was a consumer's nightmare, leaving Smallbrook Queensway as a somewhat isolated area accessed by inhospitable pedestrian underpasses, which dogged the success of this potentially important area. Forty years have passed since the shops in Ringway House were constructed, as the maturity of the trees planted at the time bear testament. Yet despite the splendid sweep of James A. Roberts's building, there has always been the feeling that this, the only part of the Inner Ring Road scheme to be lined with shops, has never reached its potential. The opening of the Middle Ring Road and the intention of the city's planners to divert through traffic away from the congested Queensway has left the 1960s road as busy as ever, but without the facility to attract even what years ago was termed 'passing trade'. Buses traverse this part of the Queensway in order to reach somewhere else, and even the lowering of the road and the consequent elimination of the Hill Street pedestrian underpass did not really create a shopper-friendly environment. The road is still catering for the motorist, although with the demolition of the buildings on the skyline associated with the Bull Ring Centre, Smallbrook Queensway's only function today is to allow vehicular access into New Street Station, although once the Bullring has been completed in the autumn of 2003 buses will have access through to Moor Street. *Birmingham City Engineer & Surveyor's Dept/DRH*

By January 1963, the changes to the New Street end of St Martin's Circus were reaching an interesting transitional point with the new road pattern of the Inner Ring Road being gradually superimposed on the rapidly fading 19th-century street model, in this case **WORCESTER STREET**. The large crane belonging to George Wimpey, the contractor, stands poised over the skeletal form of the rapidly growing Rotunda building, which would take another two years before it was completed. The siting of this tall building at the top of the Bull Ring gave the whole area a much-needed focal point and contrasted with the disappointingly rectangular block of the Bull Ring Shopping Centre. As an aside, next door to the ABC Cinema in New Street was one of the first Wimpey Bars in Birmingham, selling hamburgers. Now everyone knows that the Wimpey chain, first seen in the UK in 1955, got its name from the hamburger-chomping character in the 'Popeye' cartoons, but as an impressionable youth I thought that Wimpey's were also involved in large civil engineering products with hamburgers as a side-line!

On the right is the north side-wall of Charles Edge's Market Hall of 1835, which was still in use. It is largely forgotten today that St Martin's Circus basically followed the line of two existing side streets that ran on either side of the old Market Hall. Between the emerging Rotunda and the disappearing Market Hall, the new road on the north side roughly followed the line of Phillips Street, while on the south side of Edge's masterpiece the Ringway followed the line of Bell Street, which had been first mentioned in 1715. In the foreground is the as yet unfinished Smallbrook Ringway, and going straight on and to the left of the Rotunda construction site is the by now bisected Worcester Street. Peeking between the cranes and the Victorian Lloyds Bank building designed by F. B. Osborn at the top of Worcester Street is the 'Big Top' development in New Street. Worcester Street only came into being in the post-Napoleonic War period, having been cut through a number of dingy alleyways such as Swan Alley, The Fordrow and Ashford's Croft, and by 28 January 1963 it has itself been cut by the construction of the tunnel wall over the eastern entrance to New Street Station, which can be seen just in front of the Ford Anglia 105E estate car.

On the left are the rather strangely truncated gables of the shops that lined the west side of Worcester Street, which, from their frontages, would seem to be more at home in a suburban setting. On the near corner, in the middle of where the Station Street junction had recently been, are the derelict remains of Finlay's tobacconist kiosk, while in the block itself the first shop, with the canvas blind pulled down, is Samuel's furniture company. Next to it is the long-established premises of Fred King, who made and sold fishing tackle, while next door is the Welcome snack bar. Continuing along the block, a dark-coated gentlemen is looking into the window of Robert Morris's seed merchant's shop, and next door is Henry Woolf, watch material manufacturer. The other shop in the Worcester Street block with its sunblind pulled down (in January?) is that of Walter Glover, fruit and vegetable retailer. The shop with the long white sign belongs to the outfitter Arthur Whitcher, who

occupied the four shops numbered 31 to 37 Worcester Street. The last shop, next to the Lloyds Bank building, is Midland Red's chief booking office, which would shortly be transferred to the Digbeth Coach Station, some three-quarters of a mile away. Although this is an extremely detailed list of the shops in the remnant of Worcester Street in 1963, it does show that these small, widely differing types of shop could still survive and thrive in the city centre. Similar small, wide-ranging family-run retail outlets could still be found in Snow Hill and Steelhouse Lane until only a few years earlier, but the redevelopment of the city centre throughout the early 1960s removed many of these interesting retailers. By the time the Rotunda was completed, this turn-of-the-century row of Worcester Street shops would be ready for demolition and with it went a legacy that stretched back into the early 19th century.

The 24-storey Rotunda is a splendid building for its site on the top of the hill above **ST MARTIN'S CIRCUS**. At 271 feet tall, the cylindrical shape was a bold, possibly the boldest, architectural concept of the exciting early stages of the Inner Ring Road scheme. It was designed by James A. Roberts, who was also responsible for Ringway House and the now demolished St Martin's House in the Bull Ring. The building has accommodation for two floors of shops, three banking floors, another 16 floors of offices and two further floors of services at the top of the 'tube'. The banking and shop area is housed in the colonnaded white rustic marble slips that form an attractive base, as seen in the 1999 photograph. In its earlier years it achieved a certain terrible notoriety on 21 November 1974, when the Mulberry Bush public house, contained in the base of the building, was one of two city centre pubs targeted by the IRA, leaving 21 dead, 167 injured and many more afflicted with horrific memories and fears. When preparing this book, the writer went into the Rotunda for the first time since that evening!

If the later parts of the Ringway were totally driven by the needs of the motorist, at least the section from Horsefair along Smallbrook Queensway and into St Martin's Circus, to include the Bull Ring, was imaginative. Unfortunately the only section of the scheme to have shops and offices built along it was cut off from the rest of the city centre by the very road that served them! The Rotunda, because of public opposition, has recently survived the developer's desire to demolish it. Lloyds Bank, as one of its few remaining tenants, has remained loyal and still occupies the original lower banking floors.

In May 1999 all traces of Worcester Street have long gone, though just in front of the Travel West Midlands Volvo B10L single-decker bus is the parapet wall over the railway tracks leading into New Street Station. On the left is the rear of the Odeon Cinema in New Street, while between the cinema and the Rotunda are the rectangular blocks of the 'Big Top' site on the far side of New Street. In the foreground, to the right of the queuing traffic waiting to exit from Smallbrook Queensway, is a compass set into the decorative stones with its arrow pointing to the north, as one would expect, but also pointing directly to the line of the long-defunct Worcester Street. By the autumn of 2000 all this was swept away in the demolition of the 1960s Bull Ring. *Birmingham City Engineer & Surveyor's Dept/DRH*

The architect responsible for the Inner Ring Road scheme was Herbert Manzoni, who was Birmingham's City Engineer and Surveyor. His plans put forward in 1943 followed the earlier 1917 suggestions of having seven traffic islands around the circuit, which even when first completed in the 1960s and early 1970s were outdated and doomed to cause bottlenecks. In July 1944 the City Council approved the scheme and within the year the necessary Parliamentary Powers were obtained to acquire over 1,200 properties, 85 acres of land and an average of 80 feet of land on either side of the road so that they could have control over future development. It was not until 18 January 1957, when the original concept was already 40 years out of date, that the Ministry of Transport approved the Inner Ring Road scheme, and by the time it was only half completed, its 'noose' effect was already being recognised and the scheme was being criticised for ignoring the pedestrian and pandering to the excesses of the car. What Herbert Manzoni created was quite brilliant, but with hindsight it was flawed because it had not catered for the increased demands of the traffic even at the time of its construction.

On the site of the sadly demolished Market Hall was built an open space surrounded by bushes and trees and with a grassed area and rows of benches in the centre. This was named **MANZONI GARDENS** after the by now be-knighted Sir Herbert as a tribute to his work, particularly with the Inner Ring Road scheme, but in retrospect it was a bit of a 'backhanded compliment'. The entrance to the Bull Ring Centre by way of the escalators climbing diagonally beneath the Fine Fare Supermarket sign is in the centre of this 1964 view as people walk through or rest on the new benches when Manzoni Gardens was still pristine. Behind the large sapling on the left is the Times Furnishing building in High Street, which also housed a Burton's tailors shop on the corner with St

Martin's Circus. Passing along this elevated section of road is an Alexander-bodied coach of a Scottish operator, making its way to Digbeth Coach Station.

History has not been kind to either Sir Herbert or his Gardens. The Inner Ring Road soon began to garotte the city centre, and while making it an urban geographer's delight as a model of delineating the Central Business District from surrounding functional zones, it was soon abandoned to the pollution of the motor vehicle. The section from Moor Street through St Martin's Circus, including the Bull Ring Shopping Centre, and along to Holloway Head by way of the shop-lined Smallbrook Ringway, which the press had labelled 'the Regent Street of Birmingham', could only be reached by pedestrian subways. Over the succeeding years shoppers and pedestrians voted with their feet and stayed in the traditional New Street-Corporation Street-High Street shopping triangle, venturing out beyond that area only for the various markets, specialised shops and out of curiosity. In the 1999 picture, as if to haunt the by now doomed Bull Ring Centre, the tiled wall of the successful Pavilions Shopping Mall in High Street stands on the far side of St Martin's Queensway, as a pointer to the failure of the time-expired 1960s shopping 'experiment'.

The problem with Manzoni Gardens was that, like the adjacent Bull Ring, it could only be reached by underpasses and was surrounded by noisy, polluting traffic that even the trees didn't like. A surprising number of the original 1960s benches survived, but although it still had its grassed area, few people came to sit down in such an inhospitable part of the city. Some of the trees reached splendid maturity despite the pollution that they had to endure over nearly 40 years, and it seems a shame that after such a struggle for life they were felled with the rebuilding of the Bull Ring early in the 21st century. *Author's collection/DRH*

As a Corporation bus speeds down **ST MARTIN'S CIRCUS** off the picture towards Moor Street in July 1961, the gaping hole that was to become the open-air Bull Ring market area is beginning to take shape. It is always easy to be a critic after the event, but the planned destruction of the Bull Ring, with its impressively steep hill climbing past the Parish Church towards High Street, New Street and the city centre, was a terrible affront to the Brummie and his traditions. The construction of St Martin's Circus 'ripped the heart out of Birmingham', to quote the late local historian Victor J. Price. Perhaps it was a needless destruction, as the new multi-million-pound Bull Ring redevelopment scheme, which is due for completion in September 2003, will partially restore pedestrian access between High Street and the Parish Church to surface level and consign road traffic underground where perhaps it always should have been. On the left is the old Market Hall, in 'splendid isolation', and the incline of the old Bull Ring can be seen in the front elevation of the Doric-porched building. Immediately to the right of the Market Hall, on the skyline, is the row of multi-gabled shops that lined Worcester Street (see pages 72-3), acting as a barrier to the cavernous opening of New Street Station behind them. The construction of the Rotunda had not begun at this time, although demolition of the old buildings had been completed, allowing transient glimpses across from one street to another. To the right of the Leyland Beaver lorry, which is being let out of High Street by a friendly Corporation bus driver, is the old Lloyds Bank building on the corner of Worcester Street and New Street. This late-1890s building will itself fall foul of the demolition man's ball and chain as soon as the Rotunda is ready for occupation. The Austin FX3 taxi cab travelling down St Martin's Circus is passing scaffold-enclosed buildings that are about to be pulled down, leaving undisturbed only the tall 1930s Times Furnishing building in High Street.

The decline of the Bull Ring Centre and associated markets area over the 35 years since their completion has been painful to watch. It was obviously going to be necessary to rebuild the Bull Ring complex as its decay into a seedy, unloved, cheap-looking backwater was beginning to put a blight on this part of the city, despite the prestigious nature of the centre when it first opened in 1964. Rebuilding plans were first put forward in the late 1980s to link the Bull Ring once again with the rest of the city centre at surface level for pedestrians. Unfortunately, lack of capital and problems over the designs meant that several schemes came and went before the present development plan was adopted. The Rotunda was originally included in this mass demolition plan, but fortunately, despite all its faults, the decision was made to retain and refurbish it. Although a 'child of the 1960s', the Rotunda's imaginative design on its prominent hill-top site almost reminds one of the medieval locating of churches with their spires pushing upwards towards the heavens. It has become a focus of the 1960s Bull Ring rebuilding scheme, and into the new century it will be the only survivor of that period. *Birmingham City Engineer & Surveyor's Dept/DRH*

This further view of **ST MARTIN'S CIRCUS** in 1961 shows both the demolition of the old and the construction of the new. A BCT exposed-radiator Crossley double-decker, working on the 44 service from Acocks Green, climbs the hill behind a black-and-red-liveried BMMO S13 dual-purpose single-decker. They are passing the open space in front of St Martin's Parish Church where Midland Red services to Warwick, Stratford and Coventry had terminated until about one year before. The building beyond the double-decker is the soon to be closed F. W. Woolworth premises in Spiceal Street, which would disappear from the map. Travelling down the Bull Ring is a Bedford van, which, with its armoured windscreen, is an early example of a bullion vehicle that was, in 1961, still quite a rare sight. The truncated Bull Ring is still dominated by the bulk of the old Market Hall. The original Bell Street, which had only recently been replaced by the southern arm of St Martin's Circus, was on the south side of this huge building and had been well-known for years for its strong smell of fish. Lining Bell Street there were two public houses, the Grand Turk and the Board Vaults, one at either end, and no fewer than 25 fish-sellers, and this did not take into account the sellers in the Wholesale Fish Market, including such names as Vickerstaff, Marshall, Shipley and Normansell. The Normansell family made their money from fish and from the 1930s became a major driving force behind Aston Villa Football Club with F. H. later becoming the Villa's Chairman.

Within three years, on the site of the old Woolworth store, would be built the Bull Ring Centre, which would be one of the first American-style shopping centres constructed in Britain. Beyond the hole being created in the centre of St Martin's Circus to house the open-air market is the old Lloyds Bank building on the Worcester Street-New Street corner, while to the right of it can be seen the recently constructed 'Big Top' block of shops and offices in New Street.

The fates of two of the buildings designed by James A. Roberts have differed enormously. The Rotunda, seen in the second picture glinting in the strong sunlight of February 2000, stands above the low-set block of the Bull Ring Shopping Centre, in the deep shadows on the left. By late 2001 the Bull Ring Centre and Roberts's more traditional St Martin's House had gone. The previous reconstruction, which began in the late 1950s, took about four years to complete. St Martin's House had a life of 40 years and was a far cry from No 14, the Hobbies fretwork model shop, which, as a young lad, the author used to frequent using up most of his meagre pocket money to buy balsa-wood aircraft models.

By July 2002 the new Bull Ring Centre's framework is complete, although hidden like a birthday present behind a swathe of plastic wrapping. When opened, the glass-roofed Bull Ring will contain 130 cafes, restaurants and shops, employ 8,000 people, and have as a centrepiece a splendid twice-lifesized sculpture of a bull designed by Laurence Broderick. To the left, behind the TWM Plaxton-bodied Volvo B7L double-decker, is St Martin's Church and the indoor market hall in Edgbaston Street, while on the right is the new section of dual carriageway and, off the picture, the restored Moor Street Station. *Author's collection/DRH*

The narrow **LOWER PRIORY** linked Corporation Street, opposite Old Square and Lewis's department store, with Dale End. The upper part of Lower Priory, if that is not too much of a contradiction, contained tall, late-Victorian buildings that were a continuation of the 1880s redevelopment around the Old Square area. By way of contrast, the buildings towards the bottom of Lower Priory, near to the corner with Dale End, such as those seen in the first photograph circa 1949 alongside the Austin K2 lorry, dated from the end of the previous century and survived intact until the wholesale demolition of the Dale End area in the early 1960s. Smallwood & Sons had two shops on the west side of the street; the one with the bay window was the restaurant, and at the bottom of Lower Priory was the company's wines and spirits outlet. On the right-hand corner is upholsterer William Cook Simcox, advertising on the doorway noticeboard Axminster and Wilton carpets as well as other floor coverings.

The demolition of the King's Hall Market and the Grand Theatre next door in Corporation Street opposite Old Square meant that the huge 1930s Lewis's store and the almost new Bell, Nicolson and Lunt building development briefly stood proudly on the skyline, exposed for the first time from the south. Within a few years Maples had built a new furniture store on the site of the old theatre. The incomplete Priory Queensway, seen in the second view circa 1964, was briefly an almost continental dual carriageway, with traffic coming from Dale End and Stafford Street up the hill towards Lewis's, and down the hill from Old Square, using the right-hand carriageways respectively. Going up the hill is an almost new GON-registered Metro-Cammell-bodied Daimler 'Fleetline' CRG6LX, approaching its 55 route terminus in Old Square. On the left, the open space on the line of the old Lower Priory has become a temporary car park, containing a wonderful collection of late-1950s and early-1960s cars that includes a dual-tone Ford Anglia 105E and a Ford Cortina 113E. Standing in the distant Old Square is a Daimler CVG6 bus with a Crossley body, working on the 14 service to Lea Hall. This was before the centre of Old Square was made into the ill-fated pedestrian underpass that was finally filled in during 1998.

Well, at least they got the 'rule of the road' sorted out when the elevated **PRIORY QUEENSWAY** was completed as the main link from Masshouse Circus to Old Square; unfortunately both were both huge traffic islands standing on stilts that attracted circling traffic like bees to a honeypot. The rebuilding of Old Square back to a street-level island has certainly helped pedestrians and has been deemed a success, while Masshouse Circus was demolished during 2002. Meanwhile on 17 January 2000 a start was made on the removal of the 'hump' at the Corporation-Bull Street junction, which appears elsewhere in this book, and resulted in the organised chaos that was envisaged. On Friday 21 January, the date of the 'present' picture, the queues in Priory Queensway towards Old Square are building up ominously outside the Argos Catalogue Superstore; the left turn into Corporation Street in front of the Square Peg pub that occupies the ground floor of the former Lewis's department store building has been closed to traffic, with the result that vehicles are being funnelled into Priory Queensway.

The Lewis's building is the only recognisable link between the 1964 and 2000 views. To the right of Travel West Midlands MCW 'Metrobus' Mk II 3062 (F62 XOF), working on the 55 service to the Castle Bromwich area, is the Maple House building. The approaching Wright-bodied Volvo B10L single-decker bus is working on the free 77 service, which had been introduced just five days earlier in an attempt to get people moving around the city centre. Behind this bus and beyond Old Square on the horizon is the looming presence of the Wesleyan General Building in Colmore Circus. *Author's collection/MRK Enterprises/DRH*

Travelling towards the Bull Ring along Masshouse Ringway is BCT Metro-Cammell-bodied Daimler 'Fleetline' CRG6LX 3379 (379 KOV), working on the 50K service to Alcester Lanes End, Kings Heath. The car to the left of the bus is coming out of the Masshouse Circus underpass from the direction of Lancaster Circus. The arches of the elevated traffic island can just be seen, although beneath this the planners seemed to have run out of ideas and left a barren subterranean wasteland that was used only for car-parking by the brave souls prepared to walk through dark pedestrian underpasses and elevated walkways to reach Priory Ringway. It was a desperate place, which totally wasted a large expanse of potentially useful real estate.

The middle picture, dating from the summer of 2002, shows the remains of the Masshouse Circus underpass, which had been demolished as part of the huge scheme to develop the Millennium Point site in Digbeth. By this date the new Science and Technology Museum was well established after its move from the old Elkington's factory building in New Hall Street. A multi-million-pound scheme in Digbeth known as The East End, destined to be more extensive than the Brindleyplace development in Broad Street, was well under way when this photograph was taken. The demolition of Masshouse Circus was imperative to ensure good pedestrian and vehicle access from the city centre into Digbeth.

The third photograph, looking towards the skeletal outline of the new Bull Ring Centre, shows to the right the remains of the elevated section of the Inner Ring Road leading into Priory Circus, while in the centre is the by now abandoned Masshouse Circus underpass. *All DRH*

One wonders what a present-day police officer might say if faced with a lorry loaded as precariously as the old AEC Y-type on the right standing in **SNOW HILL**, just below the Great Charles Street-Bath Street junction, in about 1932. The lorry looks as if it might have been converted from a bus. It is loaded with furniture and is waiting outside Allsop's Furniture Showrooms. Behind it is a small Morris-Commercial 1-ton pick-up van. The descent of Snow Hill was all the more noticeable because of the ever higher wall of brick and glasswork that was required in order to maintain Snow Hill Station's level formation across Great Charles Street and the valley of the tiny Fleet Brook. Interestingly, at this stage there were still inbound tram lines going up Snow Hill, which would be abandoned on 4 June 1933, when the trams stopped using the terminus in Colmore Row alongside St Philip's Cathedral. Coming down the hill, dwarfed by the side of Snow Hill Station, is a Birmingham Corporation totally enclosed bogie tramcar, which has just left the terminus in Colmore Row. It is working on the 25 service to Lozells via Hamstead Road and Wheeler Street, a route destined to be abandoned on 7 August 1933. The tram is about to cross the Great Charles Street-Bath Street junction, which by this date was being controlled by one of the earliest sets of traffic lights to be installed in the city centre; on the extreme left, next to the young mother and her daughter standing outside Dresden's tailors shop, there is an unusual warning sign for the 'Signals Ahead'. On the next tramway traction pole up the hill towards the city is an early form of Corporation bus stop with the legend 'BUSES STOP HERE BY REQUEST'. The building with the tall clock tower on the corner of Bath Street is the impressive-looking late-Victorian Crown public house.

While attempting to stand as near as possible to the position of the 1932 photographer, a modern comparison with the earlier view is almost impossible. There is nothing left of the old Snow Hill as all the old buildings were cleared away in the early 1960s when **SNOW HILL QUEENSWAY** was constructed. On the right is the new Snow Hill Station, while between the advertising hoardings alongside the station and Snow Hill Queensway is derelict land on the line of the old Snow Hill that has served as a 'temporary' car park for at least 35 years. In the foreground is St Chad's Circus, in the centre of which is the John F. Kennedy Memorial commemorating the assassinated President. Just visible on the extreme left is a mosaic wall reminding the passer-by of the 'Age of Steam' at the nearby Great Western Railway Station, with views of that railway's locomotives down the years. These interesting features are, unfortunately, extremely difficult to reach as the only way into St Chad's Circus is by way of inhospitable pedestrian subways, which makes it another candidate for early rebuilding to street level. The tall building on the left is the West Midlands Police Headquarters at Lloyd House, built in 1963, while to the left of it is the *Birmingham Post & Mail* building in Colmore Circus, completed two years later. To the right of Lloyd House is the conical tower of the Wesleyan General Building of 1989, while beyond the top of Snow Hill Queensway is the impressive Colmore Gate office complex. *Author's collection/DRH*

Left One of the pockets of 'old' Birmingham that survived until the construction of the Inner Ring Road scheme was an area of housing and industrial premises between the General Hospital in Steelhouse Lane and Bath Street, in which was situated the Roman Catholic Cathedral of St Chad. These buildings in **ST MARY'S ROW**, which linked Whittall Street with Loveday Street, generally date from the last years of the 18th century and include, at No 1, the beautifully proportioned three-storey, five-bay house that was the St Chad's Convent and the home of the Sisters of Charity of St Paul. This Georgian brick-built former town house has a porch with Tuscan columns, and perhaps might have deserved a better fate than to be demolished and replaced by a dual carriageway! Occasionally the contrast in the uses of adjacent buildings is so amazing as to be almost unbelievable. This is one such case. Next door to the Sisters of Charity at No 2 is a 2½-storey building, also dating from the end of the 18th century, and also boasting a porch with Tuscan columns but this time with a barrel-headed pediment and larger Wyatt-style windows – and it is the home of Ward & Son, the well-known gun-makers! These buildings in St Mary's Row were originally built opposite the recreation grounds that bordered St Mary's Church, which had been on the right but which disappeared beneath the ever-expanding General Hospital during the pre-Great War period. Further down, this street led into the heart of the famous Birmingham 'Gun Quarter', and St Mary's Row contained, until its redevelopment in 1964, examples of small gunsmith's workshops in converted late-18th-century brick houses. In just one of the old converted houses alone, at Nos 8 and 9, there was the Eclipse Works of the gun manufacturer William Ford, a gun action filer, a gun engraver and a gun

barrel filer, while at Nos 10-11 was James Carr and at No 22 W. W. Greener, both of whom were also gun-makers.

A 'past and present' comparison of St Mary's Row is now impossible as it simply no longer exists. Where the Austin A60 Cambridge car was parked next to the gable end of the convent in 1964 would be approximately where the first of the cars are parked on the right of the 2001 photograph. Whittall Street, seen here, had been similarly lined with Georgian houses, and also succumbed to the redevelopers, with the distinction of not only losing its buildings but having them replaced by the back entrances to the *Birmingham Post & Mail* building and the Royal Angus Hotel in St Chad's Queensway, which is the seven-storey building beyond the ugly multi-layered car park. *Birmingham Public Works Department/DRH*

Below The remnants of Birmingham's 'Gun Quarter' straddle St Chad's Queensway. Price Street, off **LOVEDAY STREET**, was initially developed in the late 1720s, and a gun-maker who resided at No 1 in the 18th century was also a purveyor of beer. During the last century it was here at The Bull that the 'gun gaffers' paid their wages to their employees, and in this strong Catholic area of the city the local priests were often required to arbitrate in the sometimes violent disputes that occurred over money. The pub itself dates from just after the beginning of the 19th century and saw the area thrive during that century as one of the world's major gun manufacturing centres, even supplying arms to both sides in the American Civil War between 1861 and 1865. The terraced buildings beyond the Price Street turn towards Lower Loveday Street were built slightly later than The Bull, but represent the remnants of the sort of residential-cum-industrial premises that at one time were found throughout the 'Gun Quarter'. *DRH*

Above Looking over **ST CHAD'S CIRCUS** from the heights of Great Charles Street Queensway at the junction with Newhall Street on 5 September 1999, we can see the twin towers of St Chad's Roman Catholic Cathedral looking even more Germanic than usual in the bright late summer sunlight. Bisecting the Cathedral, level with the 40mph sign in the left foreground, is a Class 150 diesel multiple unit entering Snow Hill Station from Handsworth and Smethwick. The two central carriageways entering the bridge beneath the railway are actually the entrances to the St Chad's Circus Tunnel, which takes traffic on to Lancaster Circus and the Aston Expressway beyond. This section of the Inner Ring Road was the last to be finished and completed the 'circle' around the city, opening for traffic on 4 January 1971. It was the part of the scheme that had challenged the skills of the civil engineers for the first time during the road's construction, with its extensive use of tunnels beneath existing buildings such as the Council House. Because of this it enabled a reappraisal of the plans for the unfinished 1930s Civic Centre development around Baskerville House. *DRH*

Right **GREAT CHARLES STREET** was by 1967 beginning to be something of an anachronism among the new multi-storey office blocks that were being constructed around it. With the clock belonging to the printers Drew and Hopwood showing 10.10, time is running out for Great Charles Street in this form. Beyond the clock is R. S. Pearce's garage with its Art Deco-style neon sign, while next to it, appropriately enough, is Caxton House, with Imperial Chemical Industries. Britannia House is on the corner of Church Street, into which the white Bedford CAL van is going. Within a year the construction of this part of the Queensway will be under way, and instead of traffic passing up the hill it will be passing through it in the new tunnels. The steepness of Great Charles Street can be appreciated from this angle, and it is no surprise to learn that Birmingham City

Transport avoided running bus services up this fearsome rise from Snow Hill. On the left-hand side of the hill, the five-storey white-banded building is York House, which was occupied mainly by accountants and solicitors. On the right, on the corner of Ludgate Hill, the deep-roofed three-storey Victorian building with the decorative white brickwork is the M&B-owned Chapel Tavern. The tall building towering over the pub is the old Dental Hospital, where personal experience can confirm that in the 1950s and 1960s masked trainee dentists were let loose on frightened children. If I had been older, after I had my only tooth extraction done under gas, I would have gone straight round to the Chapel Tavern for several stiff brandies, though one rather suspects that many nervous adults might have done the same both before and after the extraction!

The Great Charles Street section of what was to be the Ringway was opened by HM The Queen on 7 April 1971, who inadvertently renamed the whole of the Inner Ring Road 'The Queensway' instead of just this final section. So the name Queensway, by Royal accident, was adopted for the whole scheme. Looking up the hill from Snow Hill towards the entrance to the **GREAT CHARLES STREET QUEENSWAY** tunnels on a sunny Monday 16 August 1999, the steep rise of even the present-day road can be appreciated alongside the tunnel mouths. On the right, alongside Ludgate Hill, just beneath the footbridge, is the proposed site of Birmingham's new coach station, to replace the one in Digbeth. On the left are office blocks dating from the early 1990s and ranging in style from the brick-clad six-storey block on the corner of Livery Street, to much larger units, such as the one into which the footbridge actually passes on the corner of Church Street. At the top of the hill are the multi-storey offices that line Newhall Street, while in the distance can be seen the huge glass expanse of the Hyatt Regency Hotel in Broad Street, opposite Centenary Square and the International Conference Centre. *Birmingham Public Works Department/DRH*

GREAT CHARLES STREET was named after yet another member of the Colmore family through whose estate the road was first made in the mid-18th century. It ran parallel to Ann Street, later to become Colmore Row, but because of its location a little further away from Joseph Chamberlain's Victorian town centre, it really only came into its own as the link between Suffolk Street and Broad Street to the west and Snow Hill and Lichfield Road to the north. In this capacity it became part of the national route numbering system as the A38. Great Charles Street has a level section alongside the back of the City Art Gallery before the section that plunges steeply down from the distant Newhall Street junction towards Snow Hill. On the extreme left, seen here in 1957, is Civic House, occupied by the GPO as its regional headquarters. Beyond, and set back from the street line, is the Public Health Laboratory and the Birmingham Chest Clinic, and next to it the taller Colonial Mutual Life building followed by Lombard House, both good examples of mid-1930s office block architecture. The reason for their position is that it was always intended to widen Great Charles Street, which had been part of the original First

World War proposals for a new traffic relieving road around the city centre. The distant tall Victorian block behind the disappearing furniture van on the corner of Newhall Street contains the City Estates Department building and the Garrick Club. The land set back from the road in front of the ground-floor National Provincial Bank is a car park and in it are visible a Standard 8 and an Austin A90. Parked on the road in front of the split-windscreen Morris Minor is an extremely rare Armstrong-Siddeley 234, of which only 803 were built, perhaps because of its quite awful lack of style. On the extreme right, having struggled up the steep hill from Snow Hill, is a Commer Superpoise lorry.

What is perhaps surprising is that the 1930s planners 'got it right'. In 1999 the Chest Clinic, CML building and Lombard House now stand in line with newer buildings post-dating the reconstruction of Great Charles Street to form this section of the Queensway dual carriageway. As the Travel West Midlands single-deck Volvo bus working on the 109 service heads off towards the drop down to Snow Hill and the just visible St Chad's Cathedral, there is no indication that beneath the road are the two road tunnels running beneath Paradise Circus as part of the Queensway. When the construction of this section of the Ringway was being undertaken in the late 1960s, the utmost care was taken not to disturb the foundations of those buildings that were to remain. New buildings have been built along Great Charles Street Queensway since that reconstruction and widening, which in themselves are attractive enough, but the old structures on the left have a certain harmony of style, and the interiors of the municipal offices are just as they were when first opened, reminding one of office sets in 1940s Hollywood 'B' movies! *Birmingham City Engineer & Surveyor's Dept/DRH*

SHOPPING STREETS

The development of Birmingham as a centre for 'shopping' began in the 18th century when many of the already established traders began to look for more permanent premises rather than remain in the markets area of the Bull Ring. This is not to say that shops did not exist in the Georgian market town of Birmingham, as in fact they rather flourished during that time. In medieval times the expanding New Street had in it the guild house belonging to the Guild of the Holy Cross, as well as almshouses, and after 1552 it was the home of the King Edward VI Free Grammar School, although even at the turn of the 19th century the land between St Philip's and New Street was still being farmed, suggesting that the Elizabethan New Street rather 'ran out of steam' as an important street somewhere around the present-day Stephenson Place.

The rise of 'shopping streets' in Birmingham can be traced back to the fairly obscure origins of the development of the land owned by John Pemberton. From about 1697 the selling of leases on parcels of his land led to the promotion of Old Square, Thomas Street, John Street and Lichfield Street; these were all set out in a grid pattern, which was becoming a feature of planned, rather than organic, town growth at this time. Part of Pemberton's remit was that this was to be a place solely for housing, excluding shops and any form of industry, thus promoting the area as both desirable and cultivated for the prosperous gentlefolk of Birmingham. Forty years later the Colmore family did exactly the same with the sale of their land on the Newhall Estate, and in so doing also protected it from unregulated and haphazard building. The two adjoining former estate lands therefore created along the ridge from about the present-day location of Victoria Square through to near the line of Newton Street near the Victoria Law Courts, an area of refined terraced housing with their own gardens and set in elegant tree-lined avenues. The centre for this piece of Georgian town planning was The Square, later to be better known as Old Square.

Close by, Bull Street, named after the Old Red Bull Inn, but formerly named Chappel Street, because of its links with the nearby Priory Church of St Thomas, had been the street through the town that linked north and south. Although not exactly the M6 equivalent of its day, it did see the movement of raw materials from the Dudley and Wednesbury areas of the already emerging Black Country, while animals were taken to the cattle market at Welch Cross at the street's junction with Dale End. With the emergence of Old Square, this traffic was gradually sent by alternative routes to the increasingly important market area around the Bull Ring, leaving the last market to be held at Welch Cross in 1817. The removal of this through traffic enabled the Napoleonic Bull Street to become an important shopping street.

Similarly affected by the removal of the market was High Street, which began to have purpose-built shops from about this time, some of which, for example those opposite Carrs Lane, survived until the 1950s. The image of 'chocolate box' or 'Christmas card' Regency shop windows might be fanciful, but there is enough evidence to suggest that the growth of retailing in the early years of the 19th century has long been a forgotten economic factor in the growth and subsequent prosperity of the town itself. Most workers, being paid a pittance, eked out their supplies from the markets, but there were enough ironmasters and industrialists in Birmingham at this time to support and encourage the growth of retailing in the town. As a result the trickle down into the economy of their wealth enabled Bull Street-based retailers to thrive and become part of the influential hierarchy of the town. John Cadbury, for example, opened his tea and later coffee and cocoa emporium in Bull Street in the reign of William IV; similarly it was at this time that Joseph Harris, a dyer of cloth and today a name carried by a chain of dry-cleaning shops, was set up. William Southall, a druggist who later became an important manufacturer of chemists' products, and one Benjamin Hudson, whose family was eventually to become the owner of Birmingham's best-known bookshop, were all neighbours.

Despite the dramatic decline of Old Square in the space of perhaps no more than 40 years, from a desirable residential area to the site of the worst slums in Birmingham, Bull Street managed to maintain its prestigious reputation as a shopping street of some merit. This it managed to retain until the cutting of Corporation Street in the late 1870s as part of Joseph Chamberlain's 'Grand Plan' for his 'Parisian Boulevard'. Within 15 years Corporation Street's shops had replaced those that lined New Street, High Street and Bull Street, which were to say the least somewhat basic. However, the reconstruction of New Street and Bull Street in a high Renaissance style of Flemish-inspired buildings, led by Newbury's store in Old Square and David Lewis's shop on the corner of Bull Street and Corporation Street, encouraged the further growth of retailing, so that by the last decade of the Victorian era Birmingham had taken on the appearance of a flourishing provincial town that was the equal of many other larger urban shopping centres outside London. Gone were the little Regency bow-windowed, lead-glassed frontages, which were replaced by 'emporia' contriving to sell a wide range of items that previously had only been found in individual shops. While specialist jewellers, shoe shops and ladies' and gentlemen's outfitters thrived on the ground and first floors of these new five- and six-storey premises, the age of the department store had arrived. Over the next 70 years, until the early 1960s, Birmingham could boast Lewis's, the Birmingham Co-operative store in High Street and Grey's in the then still important Bull Street. Rackham's has had the confidence to complete in June 2002 a multi-million-pound refurbishment of its sales areas, and the family-owned Beehive store in Albert Street, as well as large multi-purpose shops such as Marshall & Snellgrove in New Street, and briefly Henry's in Union Street, all thrived until the 1970s. Although C&A closed its store in New Street in 2001, Beatties took over this prestigious site, adding a new name to Birmingham's shopping centre.

The redevelopment of the Victorian-inspired retailing streets of central Birmingham was unfortunately given a 'kick-start' in the most appalling way in the early years of the Second World War when air-raids in November and December 1940, and a particularly heavy one in April 1941, caused extensive damage, destroying Marshall & Snellgrove, part of the Co-op and most of the area between them in New Street and High Street. The rebuilding of this site, still known as the 'Big Top' on account of the huge marquee that was erected on what Brummies called 'the bomb-building', was completed by the end of the 1950s, while the new Rackham's store was completed just a few years later. Yet somehow the retailing 'status quo' was and has been subsequently sustained, and 'gewin up town' to do the shopping still has some magic for much of the present-day adult population of the city and the surrounding area.

The building of the 'collar' of the Inner Ring Road has somehow preserved central Birmingham's shopping streets as the premier retailing area of the West Midlands. The hoped-for extension of the central shopping area into the pioneering Bull Ring Shopping Centre was strangled by its separation from the rest of the city centre by St Martin's Circus, and the replacement of the centre by the huge new strangely shaped Bull Ring containing prestigious department store developments such as Selfridge's and Debenhams will add to the shopping delights of the city centre. Even the opening of the Merry Hill Centre, at Brierley Hill in 1989, which had such a detrimental effect on retailing in the surrounding Black Country towns, left the importance of Birmingham's city centre largely unaffected. This has been helped by the opening of city centre shopping centres such as the Pavilions in October 1987 and the Pallasades, and the gradual pedestrianisation of the streets, all of which have made the central area shopping streets a much more pleasant and environmentally friendly area. From a few medieval stalls to the shopping canyons of 'downtown' Birmingham, the city centre has come a long way in its constant evolution, and no doubt more will occur in the near future. Watch this space!

BULL STREET got its name from the long-forgotten Old Red Bull Inn, which was situated on the south-western side of the street. By 1886 the street's oldest building, the Old Lamb House, a half-timbered structure dating from the late 16th century, had gone and the road took on the appearance that, surprisingly, it was to retain until the 75-year leases on the late-19th-century properties expired. Only the lowest building, to the left of the gas lamp standard in the foreground, was replaced between this circa 1900 view and ones taken after the end of the Second World War. In the days before the electric trams were introduced – note the lack of track and overhead – Bull Street had become a prosperous street, with Reece Brothers' tobacconist emporium dominating the corner with Dale End. Its later importance as a routeway from Corporation Street into High Street occurred rather by accident than design, as the street was rather narrow when compared to the

'planned' late-Victorian developments elsewhere in the city centre. When Bull Street was split in 1876 by the opening of Corporation Street, this part became known as Lower Bull Street. With the sun glinting on the wet cobbled street just after a rain storm, turn-of-the-century Bull Street, with its splendid gas lamps, is lined by many small shops, which it managed to retain until it was redeveloped in the 1960s. This gave this part of Bull Street a distinctly different appearance when compared with any of the other main shopping streets in central Birmingham, looking more like a suburban High Street than part of a city centre. The tall building with the twin gold domes on the corner of Corporation Street is Dean's carpet and linoleum store, built in 1886 to the designs of William Jenkins, who had obviously been influenced by Yeoville Thomason's Lewis's store just opposite, completed only the previous year. *J. Whybrow collection*

Above **DALE END** became the main A47 route out of the city towards Coleshill and Leicester under the national road numbering scheme, and its width reflected that it was here, around the 15th-century Welch Gate and Market Cross, that Welsh cattle drovers held their cattle market. Briefly, in the 1920s, a large covered tram shelter was situated about where the tram is standing in this 1948 view, and this accommodated city-bound trams on both sides. The survival of the early-19th-century buildings on the left beyond the parked 1946 Vauxhall J-type Fourteen-Six model is perhaps surprising, but their very survival into old age was a contributory factor to their being swept away. Perhaps if they had lasted for another 20 years, they might have been restored, gentrified and now be regarded as a wonderful city centre architectural gem – but the property developers got there first! The Star public house is on the left with the large M&B sign, while further down Dale End is the famous Scout Shop where one could by anything from a primus stove to an Ordnance Survey map or an Arctic survival tent. The three-storey white building belongs to Beresfords, who were early city centre sellers of televisions. Interestingly, in an upper-storey office at No 115 Dale End was the Birmingham headquarters of the Communist Party, while four Irish shipping lines were based at No 108 on the west side of the street. One of Miller Street depot's totally enclosed MRCW-bodied trams of 1923, car 643, has arrived from Perry Barr on the 6 service, and has unloaded its passengers in front of a major shop-front refurbishment – this is the London Drapery Store, which was next to Frank Platt's tailoring business. The shop with the clock over it, just to the right of the tram, is Hedges the Chemist. The tram, which is standing roughly where the present-day junction of Albert Street is situated, will move off and take the curved track in the foreground to the Martineau Street terminus. R. T. Wilson

Below During a torrential summer storm on Sunday 17 July 1949, open-balconied four-wheeled tramcar 420, built by the United Electric Car Company in 1912, travels along High Street past the **BULL STREET/DALE END** corner (seen earlier on page 91) on its

way to the Albert Street loading shelters. On the extreme left are the temporary shops that originally housed a Ministry of Food free advice centre for recipes such as Woolton Pie, but which were later used by Henry's department store until it could move into its purpose-built premises in Union Street. The rather splendid triangular-shaped building on the left, on the corner of Martineau Street and Bull Street, housing the tailors shop of John Collier, was built in 1887 and survived until 1959 when its lease ran out and the whole area became available for redevelopment, which was done by the Commercial Union Company over the next two years. This Victorian building had created something of a stir when it was built as it occupied the site of the Old Lamb House, an Elizabethan building that had survived Prince Rupert's siege of Birmingham in 1643 and was finally demolished when Martineau Street was cut through in 1886. Beyond the Old Lamb House that John Cadbury had his original chocolate factory, which he opened in 1824. Beyond the Belisha beacons – note that they are not yet, in 1949, 'zebra crossings' – and the poor rain-soaked cyclist is Bull Street. This had originally been called Chappel Street, but when it was redeveloped in the 1880s, vaguely in the favoured Birmingham-Italian flamboyant style with shops and offices, it was renamed Bull Street.

Between the curved building on the corner of Bull Street and the disappearing front end of the tram are the railings that guarded a small traffic island around which the tramcars passed on two sides. The island was in fact the roof and staircase down into a subterranean

world of glazed tiling and vitreous enamel, a urinal that, like so many in the city, was a gem of Victorian plumbing. Alas, not one has survived. To the right is Dale End, named after Dale Hall, which, during the 16th century, was a large house on the main route out of the town to the east towards Coleshill. It was not named after Dr R. W. Dale, the 19th-century Minister of the nearby Carrs Lane Congregational Church and municipal reformist – although many streets in Victorian Birmingham were named after influential local politicians. Martineau Street is a good example, having been named after Thomas Martineau, Mayor of Birmingham at the time of that street's construction. As seen in the previous photograph, Dale End widened out as it approached High Street, and even in these early post-war years had remnants of late-Georgian buildings mixed in with the later Victorian developments. *C. C. Thornburn*

By the early 1960s the redevelopment of the **BULL STREET/DALE END/HIGH STREET** area was well under way. Martineau Street disappeared when the 75-year leases for the properties expired – it was finally closed to traffic on 15 October 1960 and was replaced by the buildings constructed in 1962 that formed the eastern edge of the High Martineau Square redevelopment. The canopy on the left, in this circa 1963 view, belongs to the block that included Littlewood's new city centre store; when it first opened it had one of the first self-service restaurants in the city, and while the rest of the food was quite acceptable, the chips were some of the soggiest imaginable! The last two buildings in the block were occupied by Evans – the tactfully named 'Outsize Shop' – and Burton's gentlemen's outfitters. As already seen, the lower part of Bull Street was a narrow thriving thoroughfare with small shop units in the Victorian premises that survived until the whole block was demolished at the end of the 1960s.

The semi-circular building on the corner of Bull Street and Dale End was by this time occupied by Preedy's the tobacconist, but since the late 1880s had been occupied by another tobacconist called Reece Brothers (see page 91). For many years a sign on the corner of the shop declared it to be 'Ye Oldyst Tobaconyst Shop in Bermyngham'. Next door in the same three-storey block is one of Birmingham's first Thornton's Chocolate Kabins, and one of the Sheffield confectioner's first forays into the West Midlands;

coincidentally, it was just a stone's throw from where John Cadbury's first chocolate factory was established in 1824. The large, rather plain, four-storey building dominating Bull Street dates from the 1880s and is occupied by further clothing shops, with Zissman's tailors shop and Eve Brown's ladies' outfitters. To the right is the wide expanse of the High Street end of Dale End, where the Midland Red double-decker, one of the company's home-made BMMO D7 types, is arriving in the city centre. In front of it is one of Ford's least successful post-war models, the Consul Classic, which managed to combine scaled-down American styling with the Ford Anglia-type reverse-raked rear window. The result was a car that had the proportions of a 'camel/horse committee' design. At one time the tramcars took advantage of this wide space with a central loading island, but this was removed in the late 1920s at the same time as Henn's Walk, a narrow passageway linking Moor Street and Dale End, was abandoned for tram operation.

The 2000 view of the same spot is totally unrecognisable except for the street pattern. The tall white imposing-looking building on the skyline is the former Lewis's department store in Corporation Street, while below it in Bull Street is the Corporation Square development. Most of these buildings were completed by 1974, but for many years the Council's attempt to extend the city centre's shopping area to the north side of Bull Street had been thwarted by its poor pedestrian access; Barrow's, one of the few high-class

food stores in the city centre, had moved into new premises on the corner of Corporation Street and Bull Street, but had quickly succumbed to its poor location and from competition from the more readily reached Rackham's food hall, despite the fact that for many years Barrow's was the only place in Birmingham where one could purchase haggis! Unusually for a grocery shop, Barrow's was also agent for Sutton's seeds and Aga cookers! Midland Educational, one of the city centre's premier booksellers and stationers, struggled on until the late 1980s, but also closed its doors due to the same lack of accessibility. Salvation for the newly rebuilt area came when a new open-air market was established in Corporation Square, and it is alongside this that the Claribel Coaches Optare single-decker is parked before leaving on the long 94 service to Chelmsley Wood. The semi-pedestrianisation of Lower Bull Street encouraged a revitalisation of the street and its surrounding shops. However, Dale End, to the right of the trees, is a shadow of its former self, being mainly used as the city terminus for a number of bus services and having a MacDonald's fast food outlet opposite the bottom of Bull Street in roughly the position that was formerly occupied by the old and much missed News Theatre. *J. Whybrow collection/DRH*

Looking in the opposite direction, the **HIGH STREET** of the mid-1920s was a mixture of late-Regency buildings, such as those on the extreme right, and various styles of mid- and late-Victorian architecture. The earliest of the latter are the stucco-faced buildings on the left on the far corner of Carrs Lane, which dated from the mid-1830s, while the shops and offices on the near corner, as well as those in the distance at the New Street end of High Street, date from the redevelopments that took place in the 1870s

High Street was one of Birmingham's oldest thoroughfares. The section between New Street and Carrs Lane was originally known as High Town, while where Bull Street joined in medieval times. This was originally known as High Town, while where Bull Street joined High Street was where Welch End existed. By the late Victorian era, High Street had

developed into an important shopping street, third only to New Street and the more fashionable Corporation Street. Peeping out of Carrs Lane is a 71 class tramcar working on the 44 route from Acocks Green. The tram has been vestibuled, ie the driver's cab has windows, which dates this view quite well, as this task on the 150 UEC-built trams, which had entered service between August 1906 and March 1907, was only completed after a six-year refurbishment programme in February 1930. The tram tracks came out of Carrs Lane and into High Street before turning right again in front of the Red Lion public house into Albert Street, where the trams would load up with passengers outside the Beehive Store, the only family-run department store in Birmingham's city centre.

The redevelopment of High Street took place over a long time in the post-war period.

On the extreme right, on 17 July 1999, is the Littlewood's complex, whose store opened on 20 September 1962. Opposite is the tall 1990s block that occupies High Street up to the corner of Carrs Lane. The pedestrianisation of the section of High Street between New Street and Carrs Lane took place in 1998, but the short section towards Bull Street has limited access, officially for buses throughout the day, and at restricted times for delivery vehicles. Mark 1 MCW 'Metrobus' 2110 (GOG 110W), one of the last survivors of this type of bus and belonging to Travel West Midlands, loads up outside the due-to-be-closed British Gas showrooms. Years before, this was the site of the Oxford restaurant and snack bar, which sold the most lovely steak and kidney pies. As if to emphasise the semi-pedestrianisation of this section of High Street, there are no other vehicles in the street. Beyond Carrs Lane is Marks & Spencer, which has occupied a site in this part of High Street since the early inter-war period. Beyond their extensive frontage is the taller block of the award-winning Pavilions Shopping Centre, opened in 1989 on the site of the old Birmingham Co-operative store, while towering over the far end of High Street is the Rotunda. *Author's collection/DRH*

Perhaps one of the greatest losses in Birmingham's city centre was **MARTINEAU STREET**. On 29 May 1947 two Corporation bogie trams wait at the passenger loading railings halfway up the street outside Evans's store for the 'sizeally challenged'. This shop stood on the corner of Union Passage occupying the fairly plain City Buildings with its pilastered embellishments. On the other side of Union Passage was Alberta, a bridal gown shop. The open space on the corner of

Martineau Street and the distant High Street was a result of wartime air-raids; only the early-19th-century premises of Hilton's ladies' outfitters, in High Street opposite Carrs Lane, had survived the bombing at this time. The whole of the site from Martineau Street to Union Street was eventually redeveloped in 1962, and it was to these new buildings that Evans transferred after the loss of their Martineau Street premises. In High Street is the News Theatre. Originally opened in July 1910 as the Cinematograph Theatre, it became the News Theatre on 18 January 1932, being opened by Neville Chamberlain, then Chancellor of the Exchequer. For many years this first provincial news theatre, showing British Movietone newsreels, had Birmingham's first illuminated moving-letter sign, which announced not only forthcoming attractions but also the news headlines of the day. The cinema closed in March 1960, whereupon it was used as a furniture showroom. That left the Tatler in Station Street to soldier on for a few more years as Birmingham's last news theatre, showing a mixed fare of cartoons and old black and white comedy shorts such as Laurel and Hardy, the Three Stooges and even silent Chaplin and Keaton films. Next door is the Red Lion public house on the corner of New Meeting Street and Albert Street, characterised by its large lantern sign and even bigger clock.

Despite Birmingham's famous, or infamous, one-way system, inaugurated in June 1933, Martineau Street remained, until about 1955, a two-way street, as exemplified by the Ford Popular Y-type parked on the extreme left. On the right, the leading tram, 517, a 1913 UEC-built 62-seater, is working on the 3X service to Witton, and behind it 1928 Brush-built totally enclosed tram 781, fitted with a Fischer bow-collector, is in use on the 8 service to Alum Rock. This tram is still painted in the BCT pre-war livery that featured cream-painted rocker-panels and gold lining-out, which was omitted in the post-war livery carried by 517.

Looking up Martineau Street in the second 'past' view, the bus shelters are crowded as usual as the buses fill up with their passengers, but one wonders how many of them realise that this will be the last time that they will be able to do so in this city centre street. It is Saturday 15 October 1960, the final day that Martineau Street will be open. Not only will the buses go, in this case to the adjoining Union Street, but so will the street itself, with the expiry of the 75-year leases on the properties. By Christmas, most of what is left of Martineau Street will be a hole in the ground. The contractor's equipment is already in operation behind the hoardings on both sides: the foundations and piles for the Commercial Union building are being put in on the right, while further construction is well under way on the left on the site formerly temporarily occupied by Henry's store, which will become part of the Littlewood's complex of shops and offices facing on to High Street. Further up, the Alberta bridal gown shop is still in business on the corner of Union Passage, but this too will shortly succumb. The whole of this block between the top of Martineau Street and Union Street, which also included the rather plain building between Crooked Lane and Union Passage, was the last in this central section of Corporation Street to resist the developers. In the background, on the corner of Cherry Street and Corporation Street, is the almost complete Rackham's department store, which will open in November just in time for the Christmas trade. The bus, 1745 (HOV 745), a Leyland 'Titan' PD2/1 with a Brush body dating from 1948, is being employed on the 39 service, which had replaced the former 3X tram route on 1 January 1950. The right-hand side of the road is full of parked cars, which of course will be impossible on the morrow. The Smethwick-registered Hillman Minx Phase VIII parked beneath the rather unusual street light on the right shows that even Martineau Street in its latter years has acceded to Birmingham's one-way-street system.

The third photograph shows 'Martineau Street' in 2000! Only the service road entrance to the Commercial Union building's loading bay off High Street follows the line of this formerly important city street. The line of the kerb on the left through the entrance gates is the only remnant of the street that has survived. *R. B. Parr/B. W. Ware/DRH*

The original **LEWIS'S DEPARTMENT STORE** was opened by David Lewis on the corner of Corporation Street and Bull Street in September 1885 at a cost of £30,000. Apparently Joseph Chamberlain had suggested to Lewis that this was the prime commercial site in Corporation Street, and the resultant store was inevitably going to be a prestigious building. Lewis's first shop, with its twin towers, was designed by Yeoville Thomason, who had previously designed the Council House in Victoria Square. By the mid-1920s the success of the shop had outstripped the Victorian premises, and they were demolished to make way for a new seven-storey building designed by G. de C. Fraser in a severe classical design, completed in 1929. A few years later the block was enlarged with an extension into Old Square on the site of the old Newbury's store, which had been acquired in 1926. Strangely, the Lewis's building had a stylistic similarity to the buildings of the incomplete Civic Centre scheme in Broad Street. The free-standing Doric columns over The Minories on the Bull Street side of the store, just beyond the Brush-bodied Midland Red BMMO D5 double-decker bus working on the 107 service, supported the bridge that linked the two sites, although it was not until 1971 that The Minories were covered over by a large extension of the store between the blocks.

Lewis's was for many years Birmingham's premier department store and in the mid-1950s, when this view was taken, with its canvas blinds pulled down, it had the appearance of a series of small individual shops lining Corporation Street and Bull Street. The store also had the distinction of having some of the first escalators in Birmingham; these had

wooden-slatted treads rather than the later metal and rubber ones, and as a child the author was absolutely petrified of them, although a ride to the top floor and a walk on to the roof gardens was worth the fear of these hideous, clanking, moving staircases! Also on the roof was laid out a 'junior' road system, with zebra crossings and islands. For a small fee the parents of small children could hire one of the store's two-seater pedal-cars, which were famously expensive to buy and which were based on the design of the fairly inexpensive Austin A40 Devon. The proud feeling of pedalling one of these cars about, in those far-off days, was enhanced by having seen photographs of the young heir to the throne also sitting in one. One could also buy '99s' at the roof garden ice-cream stall, which at the time was one of the few places in Birmingham where you could buy this more usually seaside-associated delicacy. Alas, the wide-open spaces of Lewis's roof had only a waist-high parapet around them, and as a result became a well-known suicide spot. After a series of horrendous plunges, the roof gardens were closed and with them went the pedal-cars and the '99' ice-creams.

This view along Corporation Street in 1954 (see also page 12) shows a bustling scene, with pedestrians crossing from all directions. Strangely, there are no Corporation buses in sight, though there is a second Midland Red MHA-registered D5 coming up Corporation Street on the inbound 107 service from Sutton Coldfield. Prominent in front of the bus is an Austin A125 Sheerline ambulance, while the cars include a splendid mixture of late pre-war and early post-war vehicles that would have today's preservationists licking their lips!

Lewis's store finally closed its doors on 13 July 1991 and for a number of years the future of the building was very uncertain. The least likely scenario was that it would survive, but being a listed building, coupled with a vociferous campaign to keep it, that is precisely what happened. It was eventually purchased by the Richardson brothers, property entrepreneurs from Oldbury, who had been responsible for the highly successful development of the Merry Hill Shopping Centre, constructed on the site of the Round Oak Steelworks at Brierley Hill in the late 1980s. Today it is mainly offices, although the ground floor, behind the Travel West Midlands MCW 'Metrobus' Mk II in the 1999 photograph, is now a large bar called the Square Peg. The bus is turning into Bull Street over the pedestrian underpass, which replaced the earlier one-way-street layout. The underpass, with its subterranean Lewis's Record Store – which became quite well known for its huge selection of cheap classical music LPs, many on the Czechoslovakian Supraphon label – also had its own coffee bar, a bread and cake shop and a gentlemen's outfitters. Over the years, however, it became rather dingy and was replaced in 2000 in the same way that Old Square was rebuilt in 1998, by a street-level pedestrian-friendly road junction to remedy the 1960s road policy that reduced pedestrians to a troglodyte existence. Until this was completed, the projected extension of the Midland Metro Light Rapid Transit system (the new tram to Wolverhampton) from Snow Hill Station into the city centre via Bull Street, Corporation Street, Stephenson Street, then out to Five Ways by way of Victoria Square and Broad Street, would have been impossible. At the time of writing, this scheme has been approved and construction is due to begin in 2002.

J. Whybrow collection/DRH

CARRS LANE was supposedly where medieval mystery plays were performed, and the name is apparently a corruption of 'carts lane'. Although older than Albert Street 'next door', it never had the cachet of the surrounding streets, but did have the advantage of enabling traffic to leave and enter the city centre from the south. It thus became a vitally important link for the tram and trolleybus routes from the Digbeth direction, which used it as an unloading terminus. In the 'past' view, two six-wheeled trolleybuses stand humming away outside Jay's furniture shop in 1949, having come up the hill from Moor Street and unloaded their passengers. They will then run round empty via High Street into Albert Street, where they will fill up again before leaving on the long run out along Coventry Road to Yardley and Sheldon. The leading trolleybus, on the 94 service, is 36 (OC 1136), one of the 50 Metro-Cammell-bodied Leyland TTBD2s that opened the service on 7 January 1934 after the abandonment of the Coventry Road tram services. Parked outside Webb's shop is an early post-war Ford Prefect E93A, while behind it is an Austin 14 of about 1937, outside Powell's fishing, sport and gun shop, with its light stone-decorated cornices and mullions, which served as the city centre outlet for many of the companies in the city's famous 'Gun Quarter'.

The only building to survive 50 years later is Powell's gun manufacturers, which is rather ironic in view of the national ban on handguns after the shocking Dunblane massacre. The multi-storey block occupied by Dorothy Perkins on the corner of High Street dates from the 1990s, while on the right-hand corner Marks & Spencer has redeveloped the old Jay's furniture shop site as it has expanded along High Street from its original location. The Belisha beacon crossing of 1949 has been replaced by a zebra crossing, and in a radical change to the traffic flow the direction of travel in Carrs Lane has been reversed. Travelling towards Moor Street Queensway is one of the then Travel Your Bus company's Wright-bodied Dennis Darts of 1998, working on the long 97Y service to the huge housing estate at Chelmsley Wood, which was begun in 1966 and is now the size of a new town. *F. Lloyd/DRH*

HIGH STREET is one of Birmingham's oldest streets, being first recorded in the 13th century. It literally was 'The High Street', as it was at the top of the hill beyond the Parish Church of St Martin and the traditional market area in the Bull Ring. In the 19th century its redevelopment occurred in a far more patchy way than in New Street or Colmore Row. In this view just prior to the outbreak of the First World War, the buildings on the corner of High Street and New Street on the left are occupied by John Dean at ground level, while above are the offices of the Refuge Assurance Company, who are still with us today. This block was completed in 1878 and led a fairly uneventful life until 9 April 1941, the night of the last big air-raid on the city. After the raid the whole of this corner site was left a smouldering shell, and when the resultant large open space was cleared, marquees

were erected for wartime fund-raising activities, giving rise to the area being known as the 'Big Top' site. In the distance on the left, opposite Carrs Lane, are some of the Georgian and Regency buildings that survived into the early post-war years, including Hilton's ladies' fashion shop. Just visible are two top-covered 71 class tramcars, which entered service with the Corporation in 1906. On the right, above the splendid large touring car, are the offices of the Equitable Assurance Company in premises that would also succumb to the attentions of the Luftwaffe. Next door is the Birmingham Co-operative Society store, which for many years owned this classically topped building. Further down the street on the right were the premises that would later be occupied by Marks & Spencer. *Commercial postcard*

The 1950s building on the extreme right of this 1966 view of **HIGH STREET**, which was part of the Co-op site, includes the new premises of Hilton's ladies' fashion store, which had vacated their old building opposite Carrs Lane when that became due for demolition. The tall building towering above the Leyland bus is Marks & Spencer, which was completed in 1955, the previous 1920s building having been destroyed in the 9 April 1941 air-raid. The new store was separated from Hilton's by Castle Street, an alleyway that ran down to Moor Street and which had originally been a stagecoach yard for an early-17th-century coaching hostelry called the Castle Inn. Beyond Marks & Spencer is the old Jay's furniture store on the corner of Carrs Lane, which would eventually be replaced by M&S's expansion along High Street in the late 1970s. Two generations of post-war Birmingham Corporation buses are travelling along High Street towards the Bull Ring. The bus on the long cross-city 91 service is an 18-year-old Leyland 'Titan' PD2/1 with a Brush body, 1670 (HOV 670), which would remain in service until its 20th year. About to overtake it, working on the Coventry Road 58 service, is 1963-built, Park Royal-bodied Daimler 'Fleetline' CRG6LX 3298 (298 GON). The buses are passing people queuing for bus services to either Hall Green or Acocks Green.

The closure of the Co-op in the High Street on 1 February 1985 was a remarkable change in the fortunes of the store that only 20 years earlier had been one of the premier shops in Birmingham city centre. The Pavilions Shopping Centre was built on the site,

opening in 1989, while the remaining shops in the street were subject to more evolutionary change. One problem that affected High Street for many years was finding the best way for the traffic to travel; it was the subject of a number of one-way traffic schemes, with reversal of the flow from St Martin's Circus towards Carrs Lane in the late 1960s. Eventually it became restricted to buses and deliveries only, and after the 1998 Christmas shopping season buses were totally excluded. This left it as a pedestrianised area, and such was the success of the scheme that after the New Year bus services in High Street were re-instated, terminating instead in St Martin's Circus. In June 1999 the now unused bus shelters are still in situ opposite the imposing premises of Marks & Spencer. What little of Castle Street remains is the gap between Hilton's and M&S, while the dark-topped Dorothy Perkins building stands on the far side of Carrs Lane. The advantages of

the pedestrianisation of High Street are all too obvious. For many years the City Council and the local bus operators had resisted whole-hearted attempts to make the city traffic-free, despite the entreaties of many of the shops in the traditional central retail area, who realised that in order to compete with the covered out-of-town shopping centres such as that at Merry Hill, a much more pedestrian-accessible environment would have to be created – one in which the 11-ton bus could really no longer play a part. But by the time this happened, for many of the famous names and large stores that had graced the city for many years it was too late. *L. Mason/DRH*

UNION STREET was rebuilt in the first decade of the 19th century, getting its name, in 1809, from the Union Tavern, which stood in the original passageway. Looking from the Corporation Street end on 21 July 1954, the first 'past' picture shows George Brown's furniture shop on the right. This was part of the City Arcade block, one of the last arcades to be purpose-built in the city centre, which, surprisingly, survives today as a pleasant red-brick and terracotta Art Nouveau corner site. Parked outside the furniture shop is a new Fordson E83W 10cwt van; this type was in production from 1938 until 1957 and was a typical Ford of its day, having the well-known 1172cc side-valve engine, a three-speed gearbox and the dreaded vacuum-operated windscreen wipers that only worked if the vehicle was not accelerating – great fun in a thunderstorm going up a steep hill! With the exception of the bomb-damaged corner of Union Passage, which had been the site of a building known as Midland House, Union Street looks remarkably as it had done since the early years of the century. Dominating the street is the tall, late-19th-century former woollen warehouse, with its heavily pedimented round-topped windows, now occupied by Mansell's musical instruments and the dressmakers, Slendos Gowns. This would become one of the first buildings to be demolished to make way for the 'Big Top' site within the following year. Crossing Union Street is Union Passage, with Ansells' Corner Cupboard bar on the far left-hand corner of Union Street. Opposite Brown's furniture shop is one of the gastronomic gems of Birmingham – Kunzle's restaurant and cake shop, with its exquisitely carved wooden frontage. George Kunzle's were based at Five Ways and were well-known for using Trojan 15cwt and forward-control 25cwt delivery vans. But their most famous legacy, which is much missed today, was their cakes. Kunzle cakes were based on their chocolates, which themselves were

disgustingly magnificent. But, ah, who, having eaten them, can forget Kunzle's 'showboat' cakes or their Jap fancies?

The post-war rebuilding of Union Street took place in conjunction with the opening of the 'Big Top' site in 1962, and the redevelopment of the block that saw the demise of the Martineau Street area (see pages 98-9). As seen in the second, 1963, 'past' view, the main section of Union Street between High Street and Union Passage was occupied by Henry's department store, which had been in temporary premises at the bottom of Martineau Street in High Street for most of the 1950s. However, Henry's store would, like the Beehive in Albert Street, become unable to compete with the more specialised shops in the city centre and would close during the 1970s, being the first of a long line of well-established department stores such as the Co-op in High Street, Lewis's in Corporation Street and Edward Grey's in Bull Street to close their doors. On 16 October 1960, after the closure of Martineau Street, the bus services that had used it as their city terminus were transferred to Union Street, and the four buses seen here are all working on the 56 service to Castle Bromwich. At the front of the queue is 2353 (JOJ 353), a 1950 exposed-radiator Crossley DD42/7 with a Crossley H30/24R body, while the third bus is 2357 (JOJ 357), another of the same batch of 160 delivered from the Stockport-based company. Sandwiched between them is 2700 (JOJ 700), one of Washwood Heath's allocation of 'New-look-fronted' Daimler CVD6s fitted with Metro-Cammell bodies. These refined, but somewhat underpowered, buses certainly looked more modern than the Crossleys, but 2700 would remain active for only two years longer, being withdrawn in October 1968.

Union Street was radically altered by pedestrianisation in the mid-1980s. It had been obvious for many years that this fairly

narrow street, which had apparently taken over the mantle as a bus terminus previously enjoyed by Martineau Street, was not really suited for its new purpose. As a result, it became one of the first of the city's central streets to become the sole preserve of the pedestrian. The old Henry's shop is now occupied by W. H. Smith, which replaced its former Corporation Street site with these far more modern premises when the former's lease expired. Union Street is today occupied by a series of stalls, selling, for example, flowers and novelties. The buses and the crowds of waiting passengers have long since disappeared, and it has become a more thriving and far more 'user-friendly' street. *Birmingham City Engineer & Surveyor's Dept/R. F. Mack/DRH*

This is **CORPORATION STREET** in all its 'pomp'. In the years immediately after the First World War Joseph Chamberlain's 'Parisian Boulevard' had settled down to being Birmingham's premier shopping street. This new avenue joined New Street opposite Stephenson Place, and the entrance to the new road necessitated the demolition of a number of Georgian properties including jeweller J. & L. Mole and Hollingsworth's tobacconists. The replacement buildings, by now 40 years old, have acquired a patina of dirt and grime that has drifted into the city centre from the industrial hinterland, giving them a resolute feeling of maturity that belies their age.

Many of the vehicles are by this time motorised, although the canvas-topped wagon on the right is horse-drawn. On it is an advertisement for the Derby result of May 1920, in which Capt G. Loader's horse 'Spion Kop', ridden by jockey F. O'Neill, came in first. The OE-registered car that has just turned into Corporation Street from New Street dates from 1919, while one of the vans coming towards New Street appears to be a Model T Ford. The lorry on the left is steam-powered, which was, in the early years after the Great War, still a method of propulsion that retained a certain cachet in the heavy freight vehicle market. The traffic is travelling in both directions and would do so until 5 June 1933, when Birmingham's one-way-street system was introduced.

In the distance is the impressive tower of the Methodist Central Hall of 1904, while draped across the street is a banner for the Midland Musical Competition Festival, which was to be held in the Central Hall and the Town Hall. Just to the left of the banner, on the far corner of Fore Street, is an 1887 building designed with Gothic embellishments by Dempster and Heaton and occupied by Pattison's tea rooms, which survived well into the 1960s. Together with the Kardomah coffee shop on the corner of New Street and Cannon Street and Kunzle's cafe in Union Street, Pattison's was one of the best refreshment establishments in the city selling coffee made from fresh coffee beans.

On the left is the W. H. Ward-designed Queen's Corner of 1879, in which was printed the *Birmingham Daily Post* and *Weekly Post* newspapers and, in more recent years, the *Birmingham Mail*. This block was intended to give the fashionable road an impressive entrance from New Street with interesting shops such as the one on the corner belonging to Greaves, a fancy leather goods merchant. Beyond it the thriving bustle and activity of Corporation Street on this spring day in 1920 suggests that Birmingham has recovered quickly from the appalling effects of the recently ended Great War. Women in calf-length coats and cloche hats reflect the new-found independence of those early post-war years – 20 years earlier, this scene would have been dominated by men.

In 1920 Corporation Street is still lit mainly by gas lamps, a method of lighting introduced to Birmingham by a Mr John Gosling as early as 1817, but not municipalised until July 1875 under the chairmanship of Joseph Chamberlain. On the right, at the important junction with New Street, are two wonderful globe-shaped electric lights, which will illuminate the intersection far more brightly than the older gas lamps. *J. Whybrow collection*

Most of **CORPORATION STREET**, with the exception of the block exposed by the C&A sign on the extreme right, escaped the ravages of bombing during the next global conflict. The scene at 9.05am on 29 June 1950 shows Corporation Street strangely empty after the early morning rush hour and before the morning shoppers have arrived. This enables us to view Joseph Chamberlain's 'Parisian Boulevard' once again in all its glory. It had been cut through some of the worst slum properties in the mid-Victorian town centre, and created a wide, though in truth not wide enough, new shopping street. This was generally lined with five- and six-storey buildings with office chambers above the street-level shops. The old gas lamps have long since been replaced by sodium street lights hung across the street; these look good but gave a disappointing amount of illumination. Pattison's cake shop and cafe still occupies the premises on the corner of Fore Street, while on the nearer corner is Lloyds Bank, with heavy casement windows that make it stand out from the rest of the retail outlets in this bottom part of Corporation Street. The shop with its canvas blinds lowered, next door to the bank and behind the bus loading rails, is that of W. H. Smith. This shop, built in 1887, formed part of Fletchers Buildings and had a lovely 'feel' about it, being the first building in Corporation Street to be constructed with brick and terracotta, although the front was rebuilt in stone in 1921. The interior of the shop was lined with wooden panels and had a polished wooden-planked floor that creaked and groaned as customers walked on it. Nearer still is the entrance to Yates's Wine Lodge; this building, originally completed in 1881 as the Central Restaurant, had running through it the Central Arcade of shops. By the 1950s Yates's was attracting a clientele of students and 'experienced' drinkers who went for the cheaper end of the wine market. The most lethal of all the wines sold by Yates's in the early post-war period was their

'Australian White', which had a reputation of being somewhere between methylated spirit and paint-stripper, and at closing time the effect on departing customers was all too obvious. How times have changed with Australian Chardonnays and Sauvignons now highly regarded as excellent examples of New World white wines.

Further up Corporation Street, beyond the large clock over H. Samuel's jewellery shop and the disappearing Birmingham Corporation pre-war Daimler COG5 double-decker, is the Cobden Hotel, which is the building with the tall delicate tower. This was closed in 1958 and the site became the new home for Rackham's department store. The imposing white stone presence of the late-1920s Lewis's building is on the distant corner of Bull Street, while piercing the skyline once again is the tower of the Central Methodist Hall.

Careful examination of the street furniture shows a road sign that surprisingly reveals Corporation Street as still the main A34 and A41 road route, which ran straight through the middle of the city centre – remember that this was in the days before there was a need for the already proposed Inner Ring Road. Anyone who drove from one side of the city to the other and did not know Birmingham dreaded negotiating the one-way-street system, which, although easy for a Brummie, became the butt of music-hall comedians. Yet it was still possible to drive into the central area and park without restriction in Corporation Street. The most modern of the parked cars is the Austin A40 four-door Devon outside Yates's; it was the scaled-down pedal version of this car that children could steer with impunity around the junior street system in the roof garden of Lewis's department store (see pages 100-1). On the right is an early post-war Austin 10, with beyond it a Ford Prefect and a Bentley Mark VI. *MRK Enterprises*

Above As the Travel West Midlands Mark II MCW 'Metrobus' travels down **CORPORATION STREET** on the 114 service on 23 July 1999, the most noticeable feature is how little of this lower section has changed over the years since the previous photographs. Most of the original Victorian frontages on the west side from New Street as far as Cherry Street, which by a strange quirk of fate were the first buildings to be completed in 1880 in the Chamberlain 'grand design', have survived, although in many cases the facade is all that is left – still, that's better than nothing!

The only glaring exception is the C&A store, which was rebuilt on its bombed war-time site in the mid-1950s, although an opportunity was taken to set the replacement store a few feet further away from the street and therefore back from the rest of the frontages. This perhaps gave Corporation Street the width it deserved when it was originally planned in 1875 by the architects John Chamberlain and William Martin. When expansion of this building became necessary, C&A did so by building upwards, which, although producing a much taller building, managed to retain the same scale as the earlier 19th-century structures and was therefore still in keeping with the 'human' proportions of the buildings. Unfortunately, in January 2001, together with all its other British shops, C&A closed its doors for the last time. Within a year the Wolverhampton-based Beatties group had taken over the premises. Still on the skyline in the distance is the tower of the Methodist Central Hall.

The reversal of the traffic flow in Corporation Street had taken place almost a decade before. With the exclusion of everything except buses, taxis and service vehicles, officially at least, and the widening of the pavements with better disabled access, yet another city centre street has become the basic preserve of the pedestrian. Trees have been planted and Corporation Street, although not now in the style originally envisaged, has a much livelier feel about it. Unfortunately, with the frontages of the many nationwide shops and their corporate identities it could now be a street in any large town or city in the UK, having lost its 'Birmingham-ness'.

If future plans ever reach fruition, all vehicular traffic will be removed from Corporation Street and will be replaced by an extension of the Midland Metro tram service. This will leave Snow Hill Station and run to Five Ways by way of Stephenson Street, Victoria Square and Broad Street, and in 2005 will bring back to Corporation Street railed passenger-carrying road vehicles, or trams, for the first time since October 1950. *DRH*

Above right A brewer's dray rattles into **NEW STREET** circa 1895 loaded up with four barrels of beer, while the not-so-young drayman sits precariously on the back. The police sergeant on point duty, meanwhile, looks towards the top of the Bull Ring from his vantage spot to see if any more traffic is coming up that steep hill. That traffic would still be exclusively horse-drawn, though within ten years the motorcars of local manufacturers such as Austin, Wolseley and Alldays and Onions would have made their first tentative encroachments on to the city streets.

The policeman looks about 40, and it is a sobering thought that he would therefore have been a young boy at the time of the Crimean War. On the right, a large canvas-bodied wagon is being unloaded beneath the rather splendidly ornate gas street lamps. Opposite, outside the pinnacled King Edward VI High School for Boys, is a wagon whose load of crates appears to be a great danger to anyone in its proximity as it teeters precariously above the road – Health & Safety Regulations did not exist in 1895! The school had occupied its New Street site since 1552, and this wonderful Gothic building replaced the original school; completed in 1837 to the design of Charles Barry and Augustus Pugin, it served as a basis for the design of the Palace of Westminster.

The road on the left, beyond the brewer's dray, is Worcester Street. On its far corner is Albert House, occupied by drapers Turner Son & Nephew; it was one of the first buildings in the city to have a 'Georgian'-style exterior overlying a cast-iron frame. Beyond is the classically styled Lloyds Bank, built to the design of F. B. Osborn and, like those in Colmore Row, boasting a classically pillared entrance – something that banks of the time seemed to feel they required as they seemed to exude a feeling of financial confidence among their customers. Such, indeed, was the success of Lloyds, occupying this former Birmingham Joint Stock Bank premises, that in 1895 it is about to extend into the

site next door, formerly occupied by the old Hen & Chickens Hotel; in later years the Odeon Cinema would be built here.

Beyond the school is the complex of Gothic-styled premises known as Exchange Buildings, having been built for the trading of coal and other merchandise. This pinnacled building stood on the corner of Stephenson Place and New Street and was designed by Edward Holmes in 1863. Opened on 2 January 1865, it was then the largest and most impressive commercial building in Birmingham, containing offices, meeting rooms and dining, drinking and smoking facilities. It was cruelly demolished in 1965 when the rebuilding of New Street Station began. Just visible above Exchange Buildings is a rather splendid telegraph pole, reflecting the fact that the building originally contained the town's first telephone exchange, opened in November 1879 with initially fewer than a dozen subscribers.

The buildings on the right were built to the height proposed by Thomason for the whole of the Chamberlain-inspired reconstruction of late-19th-century Birmingham. They are a mixture of French Renaissance and later Art Nouveau terracotta-faced premises that included the Midland Arcade. All these buildings were destroyed in the massive air-raid of 8 April 1941. In the distance, shrouded in mist, is the spire of Christ Church in Victoria Square. *J. Whybrow collection*

In this similar view of **NEW STREET** in July 1954, the devastation caused by the bombing of April 1941 is still all too evident, with the whole of the corner site from High Street halfway along New Street to beyond Union Passage having been destroyed. Reconstruction work is slowly getting under way, having taken nine years since the end of hostilities not just to get the rebuilding plans approved, but to get the necessary finance and materials together in the almost bankrupt early post-war Britain. Because of various wartime campaigns, marquees were set up on the bombed area on the corner of New Street and High Street, which resulted in the area being known as the 'Big Top' site. By 1954 the 'bomb-building' – as all sites laid waste by air-raids were called throughout the city – was being used as a car park. The Corporation also used these sites as advertising space and put up hoardings that were a grim, contemporary reminder of death. This time it is a 'death on the road' campaign, announcing that in June 1954 the city saw five people killed and 366 injured on its roads. The parked cars on the 'Big Top' site include a Wolseley 4/44, an Austin A40 Somerset, a Vauxhall Wyvern EIX and an almost new Austin A30.

Sandwiched between it and the Humber Super Snipe Mk III is a pre-war Packard. On the extreme right is an Austin A125 Princess.

In New Street, the old King Edward VI School building has been replaced by the Portland stone-covered block of shops and offices known as King Edward's House. This was built in 1936 after the school moved to new purpose-built premises in Edgbaston Park Road opposite the University of Birmingham. Parked outside King Edward's House is a Midland Red double-decker, while beyond is the dark, soot-ingrained Exchange Buildings. Travelling along New Street is a Jowett Javelin saloon car, which has just negotiated the 'PASS EITHER SIDE' bollards, while parked next to the 'Big Top' is a locally manufactured, early post-war Austin 8 and, beyond that, a Morris Minor.

The 1998 view of New Street is barely recognisable. This section has been extensively rebuilt, the distant King Edward's House, which for many years contained the Littlewood's store, being the only survivor from the previous view. On the extreme left the Travel Shop is in the base of the Rotunda of 1965. The upper stories of the Rotunda's 'base' are occupied by Lloyds Bank, whose original premises on the corner of Worcester Street were demolished in 1971. Worcester Street, whose entrance was behind the traffic lights on the left, was closed when the old bank buildings were pulled down. The buildings on the right are part of the City Centre House complex, which was partially opened in 1956 and completed two years later. It is an unremarkable-looking building whose designers, Cotton, Ballard and Blow, probably got the bland, almost utilitarian 1950s look about right with not too many gimmicky additions that might date very quickly. A sign of things to come is that this part of New Street, normally used by buses, has been closed to traffic for the Christmas shopping period of 1998 in an attempt to counteract the effect that out-of-town undercover shopping centres such as Merry Hill had been having on Birmingham's city centre trade. Although buses resumed their operation in January 1999, permanent pedestrianisation took place the following year. *Birmingham City Engineer & Surveyor's Dept/DRH*

The rebuilt Marshall & Snellgrove store on the north side of **NEW STREET** was opened in 1955 and was among the first of the post-war premises to be completed in the city centre, although its construction had begun just before the outbreak of war. The seven-storey block was to accommodate one of Birmingham's premier shops for many years, but finally closed in 1970, re-opening later in the decade as the Centre Hotel, in more recent years the Britannia Hotel. Horne's gentlemen's outfitters was the only other building at the High Street end of this block to survive the war-time bombing, but it too would subsequently disappear to be included in the extension of City Centre House. On the extreme left is a Midland Red double-decker bus, Metro-Cammell-bodied BMMO D7 4146 (THA 146), which entered service in 1954. Parked outside Horne's shop is an early post-war Austin van, a Ford Prefect 100E, a Morris Minor Traveller with its wooden framework, and a two-door Morris Minor saloon dating from about 1953. The Victorian building beyond, on the far corner of Corporation

Street, is Queens Corner block, which was designed by W. H. Ward in 1879 and still graces that corner today.

It is surprising that the frontage of the Britannia Hotel looks a little stained in the 1998 view. Warwick Passage, hidden in the recesses of the canopy at the end of City Centre House, on the extreme right, is the only reminder of the very late Victorian retail and office block known as Warwick House. This stood on this site for barely 40 years before being demolished to be replaced by the Marshall & Snellgrove department store. The effects of the 1941 air-raid and the more recent preservation campaigns by the Victorian Society are clearly evident, with Princes Corner on the near corner of New Street and Corporation Street and the lighter-coloured face of Queens Corner opposite, still guarding the entrance to Corporation Street more than 120 years after they were built. In recent years trees have been planted, which, if allowed to flourish, will bring a touch of verdant richness to New Street. *J. Moss/DRH*

We are now looking back along **NEW STREET** in about 1935, and new Midland Red SOS FEDD-type double-decker HA 9418 is working on the 118 service to Walsall, having left its terminus in the distant High Street. Not long after this photograph was taken, the white, classically styled stone-faced building on the left, the aforementioned Warwick House, constructed to the designs of W. Thomas as recently as 1899, was demolished and a start was made on the new Marshall & Snellgrove store. This demolition made Warwick House one of the shortest-lived of the city centre's late-19th-century premises. By the outbreak of the Second World War, the new store had still to be completed and construction work was suspended. The added problems of the destruction of nearly all the buildings beyond Horne's tailors shop next door towards High Street, to the left of the bus, meant that recommencing the half-finished building would not occur until plans had been drawn up for the construction of the new shops and offices on what had become known as the 'Big Top' site. The latter work began just after Marshall & Snellgrove re-opened in its new 1930s-styled store in 1955. On the extreme right is the Gothic frontage of King Edward VI School for Boys, which is in its last year at this prestigious city centre location; the site was sold for £400,000 and King Edward House was opened just two years later, which was the same year that the new school buildings were completed on their new site in Edgbaston Park Road.

The Christmas decorations that are suspended over New Street in November 1960 in the second 'past' view are similar to the school of expanding crepe paper streamers that were hung across most living rooms during the festive season. Dominating New Street now is King Edward House on the right, which, when completed in 1938, towered over the rest of the older buildings lining the street. Parked outside the Littlewood's store is a London-registered Austin LD GPO van. Beyond is the Odeon Cinema, opened on 4 September 1937 as the Paramount. Its first feature starred Errol Flynn and David Niven in Michael Curtiz's film for Warner Brothers, *The Charge of the Light Brigade*. In 1960 the cinema's wonderful Art Deco frontage has not yet been rebuilt and still retains the fluorescent lighting on the canopy and the extravagant tower. The cinema was a real 'picture palace' with chandeliers, deep-pile carpets, decorative mirrors and occasional cane chairs and settees gracing its foyers and landings. It also had a Compton cinema organ, which survives today in Marston Green Hospital, having been removed in 1971; it was the last cinema organ to survive in the city centre.

Beyond the Odeon is the Arden Hotel, built in the last few years of the 1890s as the Hen & Chickens Hotel, while beyond again, nearer the corner of Worcester Street, is the dignified Lloyds Bank, built in 1875. The temporary shops between Worcester Street and the top of the Bull Ring, which included the Milk Bar and Steven's Bar, had by this time been demolished. Standing outside the Arden Hotel is a Birmingham City Transport Daimler CVG6 with a Crossley 55-seater body working on the long 29A route to Pheasey Estate on the Kingstanding-Aldridge border; it is being overtaken by an Austin Three-Way van. *Commercial postcard/Birmingham City Engineer & Surveyor's Dept*

The high fashions of the 1970s are evident in the garb of most of the pedestrians in **NEW STREET** in July 1978, particularly noticeable being the flared trousers. By now New Street's post-war redevelopment was complete. The lovely old Exchange Buildings on the corner of New Street and Stephenson Place was demolished in 1965 and replaced by the Birmingham Shopping Centre, later to be known as The Pallisades, which included on the extreme right a new branch of the Midland Bank. King Edward House still dominates the next block, although Littlewood's has moved out to its new store in High Street, while its former premises have been occupied by the HMV Record Shop. Just beyond this is the basement pub known as the Tavern In The Town, one of the two city-centre public houses bombed by the IRA on 21 November 1974. The sign for the Odeon Cinema can be seen beyond King Edward House, although even by this time it was being used rather more for pop concerts than for its cinematic delights. Beyond the Odeon's street canopy are the shops and offices at the base of the Rotunda. At the end of New Street, in High Street, is the 1930s Times Furnishing building, while on the north side to the left are the buildings of City Centre House, with the ground floor occupied by British Home Stores and what seemed like a never-ending row of shoe shops. On the extreme left, the old Marshall & Snellgrove store has been converted into the Centre Hotel.

The Times Furnishing building closed during the 1980s and the building was eventually turned into a Waterstones bookshop. In December 1998 the Christmas lights are again hanging across the street and the advertising sign announces that Birmingham Art Gallery is holding an exhibition of the work of Edward Burne-Jones, one of great Pre-Raphaelite Victorian artists, who was born in Birmingham. Very little has changed since 1978 except of course for the bus shelters and the lack of flared trousers. Next to the former Times building, the Birmingham Co-operative store has gone. It was sad to think that such a prosperous department store could so dramatically decline; in the early 1950s many of Birmingham's trams and buses carried on their side panels an advertisement for 'Say CWS and Save'. The savings came from the Co-op's dividend scheme – my mother's number was 15887. The old store was demolished in 1987 and replaced by the Pavilions Shopping Centre in 1989, just visible to the left of Waterstones. The 'Big Top' site on the left, despite being called City Centre House, still retains its wartime name in the minds of many Brummies; it is a somewhat sobering thought that it is already older than Warwick House that stood on this site and was demolished at about the time of the 1938 Munich crisis.

The lack of traffic is due to the temporary Christmas pedestrianisation, but just visible is Centro's publicity bus, formerly 4792 (KOM 792P), a Leyland National 1151/2R with a dual-door configuration; built in 1976 it had a short but glittering career as one of the ten buses purchased by West Midlands PTE to operate services around the National Exhibition Centre at Bickenhill, which had opened that year.
Both DRH

In the days of the horse as the means of transport, the pollution from traffic was marginally less atmospheric than today, but it was certainly more visible, as can be seen in this 1898 view looking west along **NEW STREET**. The leading two-horse double-decker bus, which is passing Needless Alley, is one of the newer 'garden-seat'-styled vehicles, where all the upstairs passengers sit facing the front. Behind it is another horse-bus, though this one has a third 'trace' horse to enable the laden vehicle to get up a steep hill. Noticeable is how all the canvas sunblinds are down on the south-facing side of the street, which, when coupled to the length of the shadows, suggests that the photograph was taken in late spring during the early afternoon. That second horse-bus is about to pass the Theatre Royal (see pages 48-9), whose canopy stands out from the rest of the buildings on the left. Behind it are the Corinthian pillars of the portico of the Royal Birmingham Society of Artists, built in

1829 to the designs of Thomas Rickman and Henry Hutchinson and demolished in 1911 due to rising costs and a falling revenue – now where have we heard that one before? The lone cyclist pedals past the policeman who is looking down Lower Temple Street towards the distant barrel roof of New Street Station. By the last years of the 19th century much of the rebuilding of New Street, from a Georgian central town street into the impressive shopping street that has largely survived today, had taken place. Pockets of Regency buildings at the bottom of Temple Street and Bennetts Hill had survived, but would be demolished in the next decade, except, strangely, the building on the corner of Temple Street, whose first floor is occupied by Allwood's dentist surgery. This small, elegant building has somehow managed to survive into the 21st century.

The second 'past' view takes us to circa 1946, and from Yeoville Thomason's impressive buildings near the corner of Corporation Street, the view along New Street, or, as the Brummie would have put it, 'up New Street', towards the Town Hall, is strangely devoid of traffic. The *Birmingham Post* building stands next to Cornish Brothers' wonderful bookshop, while guarding the entrance of Cannon Street on each corner are two gentlemen's outfitters, Hope Brothers next to Cornish's and Austin Reed opposite. Just beyond is the Kardomah Café, with its Art Nouveau woodwork and beaten copper fitments. It was here at the turn of the century that the soon-to-be-famous actress, Sybil Thorndike, met her actor-manager husband Lewis Casson. A motorcycle combination has crossed the Temple Street junction, while to the left, demonstrating the one-way-street system, is a large Wolseley car. Behind them is a pre-war Birmingham City Transport Daimler COG5 double-decker bus, loading up with passengers outside the J. Lyons Café and the large Woolworth's Bazaar. At the far end of New Street, framed by the Town Hall, is a wartime Guy 'Arab' II bus, which at this time would probably still have been fitted with its dreaded wooden-slatted seats. On the extreme left is the old Midland Bank, while next door is the canopy of the Midland Hotel. Just visible is the entrance to Burlington Passage with the 'high-class' Morgan & Ball's shirt shop on the far corner. The upper part of New Street escaped the ravages of the wartime bombing, except for the

Bennetts Hill corner site, which can be identified by the large white hoarding halfway up New Street on the right, near the bus. This site would receive the first post-war city centre building in the form of Shell-Mex House, opened in 1953 (see page 124).

By 2000, because of the pressure from the Victorian Society in Birmingham, many of the buildings that in previous years would have been swept away are now apparently saved, though in all honesty it is only the facade that remains. The 1879 *Birmingham Post* building was vacated by the newspaper company as long ago as in 1965 when its new premises in Colmore Circus were opened, and the Stephenson Chambers building next door, designed by Essex, Goodman and Nicol to replace a number of Georgian premises in 1899, was restored in the early 1990s. The fabulously Dickensian bookshop of Cornish's disappeared at the same time as the newspaper moved, being taken over by Hudson's. The block survives as an excellent example of how preservation can be made to work successfully. That on other side of Cannon Street is also undergoing refurbishment. On the extreme left is the former Midland Bank, built in 1869 and thus predating the grandiose Chamberlain plans for the city centre. It was designed by Edward Holmes in a restrained classical style with an entrance with marble Ionic columns rather than the Italian Renaissance style that figures so prominently in the buildings opposite and along most of Corporation Street. After the Midland Bank's overseas branch vacated these premises, the Grade II listed building was converted into a bookshop. Next door is the Midland Hotel and Burlington Passage, both of which have been rebuilt and altered out of all recognition, causing the disappearance of most of Burlington Arcade. Further up New Street is the tall glass extension to the Woolworth building, while through the trees in the distance are the columns of the Town Hall. After more than a century of bustle with horses, carriages and carts, cars, vans and buses, today pedestrians are able to walk and shop without dodging vehicles in what had become an ever-more-congested city centre. It could be argued, however, that today New Street looks like the main street in every other provincial city or town. *Commercial postcard (2)/DRH*

The flashing pen sign on the corner of Pope's stationery shop marked the junction of **NEW STREET** and **LOWER TEMPLE STREET**. This corner site contained 13 shops, of which nine faced New Street, as well as the entrance to Burlington Chambers; just to the left of Pope's in this Wednesday 23 June 1954 view is Day & Company's boot and shoe shop, while next door again was the famous and long-lamented Hudson's bookshop. However, it was H. P. Pope's shop that was the real treasure trove, being famous until its closure in the 1970s for its showcases of fountain pens, including those made by Conway Stewart, Swan, Waterman and Parker. Pope's had a wonderful smell of leather briefcases, wallets and bags, an aroma that could also be experienced at the other large stationers in the city centre, Stanford & Mann. Both supplied paper, ledgers and notebooks to the many offices and shops throughout Birmingham in the days before the invention of the photocopier, word processor and fax machine. A by-product of all this paper was that both Pope's and Stanford & Mann also sold filing cabinets and storage boxes. Next door in Lower Temple Street is another department of Day's shoe shop, which is next to Pullars of Perth, a dry cleaners. The block ends at Burlington Arcade, where such hidden delights as Margoschis's stamp dealing emporium were situated. At the bottom of Lower Temple Street is the already unloved and soot-encrusted frontage of the Queen's Hotel in Stephenson Street, attached to New Street Station and opened at the same time as the station in 1854. Originally owned by the

London & North Western Railway, its telegraphic address, 'BesthotelBirmingham', rather said it all! After years of post-war neglect, this once elegant hotel was closed on 31 December 1965 and was finally put out of its misery in 1966 during the rebuilding of the station. This also coincided with the electrification of New Street's railway lines as part of the West Coast Main Line scheme from London Euston to Glasgow. The vehicles in Lower Temple Street include a Fordson E83W van, a Vauxhall Velox EIP, an Austin A135 Princess and a Hillman Minx Phase III, which are all parked in the restricted No Waiting Zone that already existed at this time.

The whole of the block that included Burlington Arcade was extensively renovated in the first half of the 1990s. The retention of the buildings was in no small part due to the change in the Corporation's policy regarding retaining Victorian structures, by making the street frontages at least listed buildings in the New Street conservation area. The rebuilding of the Midland Hotel certainly enhanced the area, but the loss of the Atkinson Bar in Stephenson Street and Burlington Arcade is to be lamented. The wonderful fountain pen sign on the corner, together with its owner, H. P. Pope, had long gone by 1998, the occupier now being Karen Millen, a ladies' dress shop. The gap between the two blocks in Lower Temple Street, which was Burlington Arcade, has been filled in with a glass-fronted section, but this has left the city without yet another of its alleyways. By February 1970 the old Queen's Hotel building had been replaced by the 94-unit Birmingham Shopping Centre, now renamed The Pallasades, and the ten-storey Exchange Buildings office block above New Street Station. The whole of this redevelopment, including the reduction of New Street into a 'semi-underground' station with a raft of commercial development above it, has been a constant source of criticism, as, rather like the now-demolished Bull Ring Centre, it was too much, too big and too inaccessible to be much of a success.

When writing a book of this nature, it is far too easy to fall into the trap of looking at the old, the departed and the forgotten through rose-coloured glasses. Not everything that was demolished in Birmingham's city centre in the 1960s was necessarily worthy of retention, but it has to be said that many of the replacement buildings, such as that above New Street Station, were products of their time and displayed all too quickly everything that was wrong in terms of accessibility and scale. The grace and style of the Victorian buildings, such as these in Lower Temple Street, which in truth are nothing remarkable, easily outweigh the architectural blunders that frequently replaced them.

Birmingham City Engineer & Surveyor's Dept/DRH

One of the first post-war buildings in the city centre to be completed stood on the corner of **NEW STREET** and **BENNETTS HILL**. This was Shell-Mex House, opened in 1953. The corner had been damaged in a wartime air-raid and efforts were made by the Council to build on these gaping city centre holes as quickly as possible. Thus Shell-Mex House for the Shell-British Petroleum group became the first of a series of mid-1950s in-filling redevelopments. The completion of Marshall & Snellgrove's pre-war building, the C&A store in Corporation Street and the rebuilding of Marks & Spencer in High Street were all on individual sites. Only the biggest redevelopment at this time was anything like comprehensively planned, and that was the 'Big Top' construction on the corner of High Street and New Street. The Shell-Mex building was designed in 1951 by Cotton, Ballard and Blow, who were also responsible seven years later for the Woolworth Building on the site of the old Theatre Royal. The ground floor was occupied from new by Barclays Bank, although for many years a combined office and information shop for the British Overseas Airways Corporation and British European Airways occupied the New Street side of the development, which had in its window a series of rather superior models of the latest airliners in their respective fleets. From Boeing Stratocruisers to Vickers Viscounts, and from de Havilland Comets to the 'Whispering Giant', the Bristol Britannia, models of the latest aircraft were all displayed until obsolescence, an air crash involving a real aircraft of the type, or a new type of airliner caused one of the types to be replaced. The last model was of a Hawker Siddeley Trident, which arrived in the window in the early summer of 1964. The rest of the building, with its zig-zagged angled windows on the New Street face, and alternate windows with window boxes on Bennetts Hill, and the unusual concrete canopy overhanging the roof, were very distinctive features. It was also built a few feet further back from the Woolworth bazaar next door, on the other side of Fire Office Passage, with a view to the possible rebuilding of other properties in New Street on a new, wider alignment, which never took place.

The ground floor of Shell-Mex House is still occupied by Barclays Bank, although BOAC and BEA have long since gone – whatever happened to their beautiful aircraft models? The building, which Nikolaus Pevsner describes as having a 'very restless facade', has, unlike many of its early post-war contemporaries, stood the test of time remarkably well. It looks like a building from the end of the Art Deco period, and its attention to detail is a refreshing factor in making it look different from the slab-sided, uncompromising blocks that followed it. Seen again in the summer of 2000, having recently been renovated and cleaned, Grosvenor House, as it is now called, remains a uniquely styled city centre building. *J. Moss/DRH*

In 1957 Joe Moss, a well-known local railway modeller, took a series of photographs of the buildings in New Street to assist him in the making of dioramas and model buildings for large OO-gauge model railway layouts, and what has survived is a very nostalgic look back into the 1950s. This was a period before the large-scale post-war redevelopment of the city had taken place, and he captured detailed views of buildings that have either been demolished or have dramatically changed either at street level or internally. Next to Fire Office Passage in **NEW STREET**, behind the bus stops on the right and beyond the still new Shell-Mex House, is a line of buildings that replaced late-Regency structures, which included the original premises of the Royal Birmingham Society of Artists. This impressive 1829 building had a carriage portico with four Corinthian columns, but was demolished in 1911 and replaced by the building seen here alongside the Fordson 5cwt EO4C van. The new building was named New Street Chambers and was continued in a similar vein down New Street to Fire Office Passage by another, longer ten-bayed office block, the ground floor of which for many years contained one of the central area's numerous Woolworth's stores. The man on the first-floor window ledge above the store is not attempting to end it all, but is in fact cleaning the canvas blinds of one of Birmingham's numerous Joe Lyons Corner House restaurants. Outside Woolworth's is a late pre-war Wolseley saloon, either an Eighteen or Twenty-One, which is beginning to look its age. At the top of New Street, beyond Christ Church Passage, is the darker stonework of Central House, which is being passed by a 1948-built Birmingham City Transport Brush-bodied Leyland 'Titan' PD2/1. This bus has just come out of Hill Street and is working around the city centre one-way-street loop, having come in from Yardley Wood on a 13A service.

Yet again, much of New Street has managed to escape the ravages of reconstruction, but it has nevertheless had its character dramatically altered by the exclusion of vehicles. On a November day in 1998, with a low, bright sun casting deep shadows over the pedestrianised street, the old Woolworth store and the Lyons Corner House have long since been replaced by a variety of novelty card shops, sandwich bars, a Pizza Hut and Blue Arrow's personal financial services office. The cleaned-up facade of the building, next to Grosvenor House, makes a dramatic impact in the late afternoon sunlight and shows what can be done to an old building if it is given a certain amount of 'TLC'. *J. Moss/DRH*

The triangular building dominating this 31 July 1956 scene occupies a site bounded by Pinfold Street in the distance, **NAVIGATION STREET** to the left and **STEPHENSON STREET** to the right. The strange shape of this 1880s building is a throw-back to the development of New Street Station. When it was first proposed by the London & North Western Railway in 1846, the only buildings that would disappear included the old Town Gaol, three chapels and most of the worst slum houses in the centre of the town. It also meant the removal of most of Pinfold Street, The Froggery, Peck Lane, King Street, part of Lower Temple Street, Colmore Street, Queen Street and Vale Street. Pinfold Street crossed the site of the station and joined Dudley Street at its junction with King Street, which was roughly on the line of present-day Stephenson Place, but was about double the present road's length. Queen Street, which ran parallel to Pinfold Street, also crossed the site, entering Peck Lane halfway down towards Dudley Street. New Street Station, together with the contemporary Queen's Hotel development along Stephenson Street, opened on 1 June 1854, and left both Lower Temple Street, to the right of the traffic bollards, and Pinfold Street mere shadows of their former selves. Navigation Street had only been built following the 1769 opening of the Birmingham & Wolverhampton Canal, which had been a product of an earlier transport revolution. With the widening of Ethel Street to Pinfold Street in 1875, which is where the front of the Corporation bus is just visible on the right up Stephenson Street, this triangular site was created for development.

The resulting Guildhall Buildings is pleasing because of its unusual, yet regular shape. The majority of the corner site is occupied by Reid Brothers, a gentlemen's tailor. Parked outside the shop in Navigation Street is a 1933 OC-registered Austin Ten convertible. OC was the last of the two-lettered registration marks issued by Birmingham's Motor Taxation Office, and was somewhat out of sequence as OA had appeared in 1913, OB in 1916 and OE after the end of the First World War (OD was a Devon registration). Beyond the Austin and next to the double-parked British Railways three-wheeled Scammell Three-Ton Mechanical Horse is an early post-war Austin Ten, while following Midland Red BMMO D7 bus 4129 (THA 129), working on the 137 service to Halesowen, Brierley Hill and Gornal Wood, is a Ford V8 Pilot. In Stephenson Street there is a selection of post-war cars that would make a present-day preservationist's mouth water! These range from an almost new Ford Popular 103G of 1955 to a whitewall-tyred Hillman Minx Series I, which looks as if it has come from a different age from the 'sit-up-and-beg Ford 'Pop'. On the right, the Theatre Royal has a production of *Glamorous Night* during this, its last season. As with many theatres, the bare, extremely utilitarian rear contrasts enormously with the enticing box-office entrance in New Street.

How Guildhall Buildings has survived the rebuilding in this part of the city centre is something of a minor miracle! Only the Piccadilly Arcade, on the extreme right, and ABC's long-closed New Street Cinema have managed to survive. The triangular building was extensively renovated in the late 1970s, but not long afterwards much of the corner of Pinfold Street and Stephenson Street was destroyed when a fire broke out in a large Indian restaurant. Subsequently, in the mid-1990s a West Midlands double-decker bus embedded itself in a shop front in Stephenson Street, causing substantial structural damage. Yet here it is, Guildhall Buildings, still intact and thriving in July 1999! Virtually all the shops have changed hands, with the loss of Horton's toy shop and the West End Stamp Company, while Reid Bros has been replaced by a succession of clothes shops, the last being Nicholls, which itself appears to have closed down. The Woolworth building and Churchill House have also seen large changes since they were opened in 1961, but it is the use of this section of Stephenson Street that has changed most. Today, for the first time, it is the terminus for a number of Travel West Midlands bus services, and will eventually take the extended Metro tram line up to Paradise Circus and Victoria Square. *Birmingham City Engineer & Surveyor's Dept/DRH*

OLD SQUARE was developed after John Pemberton purchased the site in 1697 and laid it out as an elegant Georgian square, and throughout the 18th century it had a reputation as one of the most sought-after addresses in the town. Old Square was situated on a line from Temple Row, leading from the newly built St Philip's Church to Lichfield Street, which was the main route out of the town to the north-east. The square managed to keep its prestigious reputation for more than 100 years. Originally shops, workshops, pig-sties and 'dung hills' were excluded from Old Square, but gradually, by the mid-19th century, its status declined. Although many of the original buildings survived into the 1880s as offices, the construction of Corporation Street, begun in 1876, spelled the end for this elegant square.

By the date of the first of these three 'past' views, about 1890, the northern side of the square, next to Upper Priory, was ready for demolition in favour of a proposed 'Winter Gardens and Exhibition Hall', which was never built. Instead, another large Flemish, mock-Gothic five-bay block of offices was erected. This obliterated the 'squareness' of this corner of Old Square by taking a straight line from Upper Priory to Corporation Street. On the extreme right are the offices of Birmingham Central Tramways, one of the first operators of public service vehicles in Birmingham. By 1890 BCT was responsible for steam tram services to Kings Heath, Sparkhill, Small Heath, Saltley and Perry Barr, a horse-tram service to Nechells, the cable tram route to Hockley and the New Inns on the Handsworth boundary, and, within a year of this photograph, the accumulator tram route along Bristol Road to Bournbrook. This was the most successful and long-lived battery-powered tramcar route in Britain. Clustered around the magnificent gas light in the centre of Old Square are a number of barrow-boys with their wicker barrows, who appear to be gossiping rather than selling any of their wares.

By the middle of the last decade of the 19th century, only a few of the Georgian buildings, which had been the epitome of the wealth and style of the well-to-do Birmingham businessman, survived in Old Square, and these were about to disappear after a long period of decline. Dominating the western side of the square in the second, circa 1898, photograph is Newbury's huge department store, built in 1896 to the design of Essex, Nicol and Goodman in red terracotta and graced with, for the time, huge shop windows to display the store's products. Opposite, the old BCT building has been replaced by another of Essex, Nicol and Goodman's buildings, which would last until the early 1960s when it would be replaced by a six-storey block that would sweep along Priory Queensway and into Old Square. Newbury's extravagantly styled building had three large cupola towers on the roof, which distinguished it from those surrounding it. Newbury's was purchased by Lewis's in 1926 and subsequently demolished when Lewis's extended its Bull Street premises. By the 1890s Old Square had become a turning circle for a number of steam tram services operated by City of Birmingham Tramways (CBT), successor to BCT after the reformation of the company on 26 September 1896, and by the Birmingham & Aston Company, which ran to Perry Barr and Aston Cross. Here, one of the B&A Kitson steam tram locomotives waits with its double-deck trailer at the loading-up point before turning left into Corporation Street and proceeding to Perry Barr. On the left are the entrances to the ladies' and gentlemen's public toilets, which survived until the 1960s. These had tiled walls, vitreous urinals and cubicles with wooden doors so thick that they would have done justice to a castle under siege!

The third view is dated March 1932, and the doomed Newbury's building now sports Lewis's name as one of the new trolleybuses, 11 (OV 4011), loads up with passengers in Old Square. All the men are wearing some sort of headgear, while most of the women have heavy winter coats, some with fashionable fur collars. The centre island is just visible to the left of the trolleybus and has acquired a classic Gilbert Scott-designed telephone box. The original Nechells horse-tram service, the last in Birmingham, went on New Year's Eve 1906, while the electric tramcars, which always terminated in Martineau Street, lasted until 1922, when the Nechells electric service was the first in the city to

be abandoned. After more than 23 years as a terminus for the steam tram services, after their demise, when the CBT leases expired, Old Square remained without public transport from 1907 until 1922. When the Nechells trolleybus route opened on 27 November 1922 it was the first in the country to be operated by a fleet of closed-topped double-decked vehicles. These 'solid-tyred', outside-staircased Railless trolleybuses had a long innings, but after ten years' service were becoming as old-fashioned as the trams they had replaced. The introduction of a new fleet of trolleybuses in the first week of February 1932 'revolutionised the revolutionary'; the 11 new Leyland TB2s were the Lancashire company's first essay into trolleybus manufacture largely at the behest of Birmingham

Corporation's management and the local GEC Company in Witton, which was looking to open up new markets for its electric traction motors. One peculiar feature about these Short Brothers-bodied trolleys was that they had motorbus-style half-cabs alongside a bonnet that not only had a chromed radiator, but also a water filler-cap that apparently opened! The trolleybuses originally displayed 'NECHELLS 7' on their destination roller-blinds, but they were found to be overweight. As a result they lost seating capacity, and further slimming down lost them their roller-blinds, leaving the destination display as a paper one that just read 'NECHELLS'. *J. Whybrow collection/ commercial postcard/Ribble Enthusiasts Club*

Newbury's shop in **OLD SQUARE** was taken over by neighbouring rival Lewis's in 1926, and in 1932 the old building was demolished and the construction of Lewis's extension on the Steelhouse Lane side of The Minories was begun; on the left the huge steel frames for the new store have been erected along Upper Priory. This photograph can be dated fairly precisely, as beyond the gabled old hospital buildings and just to the right of the large trolleybus traction pole next to the entrance to the toilets, carrying the AA sign for Temple Street and Waterloo Street, can be seen the Gaumont Cinema in Colmore Circus. This opened on 9 February with Ronald Colman, that most debonair of British romantic actors who had succeeded in Hollywood, starring as the gentleman cracksman in the 1930 film *Raffles*. The buildings on the right are occupied by Bell, Nicolson & Lunt, who were wholesale drapers and warehousemen. Old Square's shops also include Decorwall's wallpaper shop and Withers cafe, which would survive until the early 1960s when the new premises for Bell, Nicolson & Lunt were built along the newly aligned Priory Queensway. As already mentioned, 1932 would see a dramatic change in the trolleybuses used for the Nechells service, but typically there is not one in sight! The subterranean Victorian toilets, which were first 'excavated' in the 1890s, remain beneath their small island in the middle of Old Square's face with Corporation Street and are magnificently illuminated by the wonderfully decorated double lamp-post.

From the middle of the 1960s until 1997 Old Square was a traffic island with pedestrian subways and shops in the open space beneath the gyratory system. For many years one of the city's premier butchers shops, City Butchers, occupied one of these semi-subterranean units, but because of the gloomy access tunnels, gradually all the shops in this central space closed and it became a graffiti-defaced place best avoided. By 1998 Old Square has been transformed: the 'hole-in-the-ground' shops have been demolished and the space filled in so that once again pedestrians can cross from one side of the square to the other at street level. Dominating the newly revamped area is a memorial to one of Birmingham's more famous sons. The city has spawned many comedians, including Tom Costello, a turn-of-the-century music hall artist, the great Sir George Robey, billed for more than 40 years as 'The Prime Minister of Mirth' and the first music hall comedian to be knighted, and Sid Field, who was born in Osborne Road, Sparkbrook, and died at the tragically early age of 46 in 1950. Latterly, the Birmingham comedian's mantle has been carried by Don Maclean and Bob Davis, better known as Jasper Carrott. However, it is perhaps Tony Hancock who is best remembered. Born in Southam Road, Hall Green, on 12 May 1924, his *Hancock's Half Hour* programmes on BBC radio and television, written by Ray Galton and Alan Simpson, created a world based around 23, Railway Cuttings, East Cheam, and as situation comedy it has never been bettered. Tony Hancock committed suicide on 25 June 1968 in an Australian hotel room, leaving the poignant note that 'Things seemed to go wrong too many times'. Belatedly his genius has been recognised and the steel silhouette statue of him in Old Square, with his trilby hat and astrakhan-collared coat, is a fitting tribute to his memory. Behind the statue is the former Bell, Nicolson & Lunt building of the 1960s, while beyond Priory Queensway, in Colmore Circus, is the 1989-built premises of the Wesleyan General Assurance Company, extended over the site of the old Gaumont cinema, which finally closed its doors on 29 October 1983 after a showing of the film *Yellowbeard*. The cinema lay derelict for over five years before being demolished in 1988. *Author's collection/DRH*

On Thursday 14 May 1931 one of Birmingham's original Railless F12 trolleybuses with outside-staircase bodies built by Charles Roe in 1922 approaches **OLD SQUARE** along **CORPORATION STREET**, having worked into the city from Nechells. These 'solid-tyred' trolleybuses, including this one, 11 (OK 4833), had a surprisingly long life, but by 1932 all of the batch of 12 would be withdrawn. The Washwood Heath depot drivers of these early 'trackless trolleys' really earned their 'corn'. They had tram-type hand controllers, which meant that they had no foot accelerators. Driving them was a real art: as well as their speed being controlled by hand, they also had to be steered, which must have been really hard work with their solid tyres. The 1930-registered Austin Seven in the foreground is travelling out of the city towards the Victoria Law Courts, and will pass the tall graceful tower of the red-brick and terracotta Methodist Central Hall. This dates from 1903 and represents the last part of the development of the Victorian plans for Corporation Street. On the right is the Kings Hall, which opened in September 1907 as a music hall; it became Birmingham's first permanent cinema in 1910, but closed down in about 1932. It subsequently became a market, in which capacity it served for the majority of its life. Next to it was the Grand Theatre, whose large auditorium had a capacity for 2,200. This was much older than the Kings Hall, having opened on 14 November 1883; it was taken over by Moss Empires in 1907, and on 1 September 1930 it re-opened as a cinema showing the classic Lewis Milestone film *All Quiet on The Western Front* starring Lew Ayres, Louis Wolheim and John Wray. This was one of the first films to show the futility and ghastliness of war and showed how a generation of young men had been wiped out during the recent Great War. Despite starting its new career with such an epic film, the Grand closed less than three years later on 13 May 1933, and after being empty for a few years it re-opened in its third incarnation, this time as Mecca Dancing's Grand Casino Ballroom. This closed in 1960 and the whole block was demolished as part of the Priory Queensway redevelopment scheme.

The sad decline of the Kings Hall and the Grand Theatre led to this section of Corporation Street becoming, by the late 1950s, perhaps the shabbiest part of the street. The Art Nouveau cornices above the church-like Gothic windows of the Kings Hall reveal that the building was intended for more intellectual pursuits than the old Navy game of 'housey-housey'. The main entrance to the cinema was in Lower Priory, on the extreme right, where the tobacconist's kiosk displaying the sign for Player's cigarettes is situated. The entrance to the foyer in Corporation Street was through the round arch with its wooden doors. Parked outside Blake's medical store and Saunders opticians, whose canvas awning is lowered on this sunny day in the summer of 1959, are two Mark II Ford Consul 204Es. The

leading one is an original Mark II model, while the two-tone one behind is a Mark II 'lowline', an updated version introduced in February 1959. Beyond is the block of buildings occupied by Maples house furniture store, which had a highly improbably polished marble frontage. The next block with the large clock on its wall on the distant corner with James Watt Street is Gazette Buildings, occupied by the *Birmingham Gazette & Despatch* newspaper. Almost inevitably, the tower of the Methodist Central Hall dominates the rooftops beyond James Watt Street in the lower part of Corporation Street. Through the wrought-iron railings of the toilet entrance on the traffic island in Old Square can be glimpsed one of Birchfield Road Garage's early post-war Daimler CVA6s buses working on a shortworking of the 29A service from the Circle at Kingstanding towards High Street with the fairly anonymous destination display of 'CITY'.

On 23 July 1999 Tony Hancock's silhouette faces along Corporation Street, having been moved from its original position on the pavement below the old Lewis's store on the Old Square-Corporation Street corner. On the base of the statue is the inscription 'I do not think I ever met a man as modest and humble'. The filling-in of Old Square back to street level has certainly enhanced what had become a rather 'seedy' area of Corporation Street. On the right is the five-storey Maples House, named after the furniture store that originally occupied the ground-floor shops that are now used by the RSVP clothes shop. Above Hancock's trilby hat is the only building to survive between the old Lower Priory and James Watt Street from the previous photograph taken 40 years earlier. This is Gazette Buildings, which was vacated by the Birmingham newspaper shortly after the *Birmingham Post & Mail* building in Colmore Circus was opened by the late HRH Princess Margaret on 26 October 1965. Still gracefully omnipresent is the Methodist Central Hall with its campanile red-brick tower. *Author's collection/J. Whybrow collection/DRH*

In the last years before the outbreak of the First World War the climatic records reveal that the first years of the 20th century enjoyed generally above-average temperatures in the summer months, and this is reflected in the photographs of the time, which are apparently nearly always bathed in sunshine. It was almost as if this was a natural 'honeymoon' before the horrors of the Great War and the destruction, loss of life and appalling weather conditions that would bring so much havoc and death in the mudfields of Flanders. **CORPORATION STREET** in 1914 was the retail heart of the developing Birmingham, and down it trundles an open-top tramcar from the 221 class built by UEC in 1906, having left its Martineau Street terminus, which is where Dunn & Company's gentlemen's outfitters is situated on the right. Beyond it, immediately below the tower of the Methodist Central Hall, is one of the original 1-20 class top-covered trams known as the 'Aston bogies', which is working on the service to Perry Barr. The post-box in the foreground stands in the section of Corporation Street between Martineau Street and Union Street, which was a far less important thoroughfare than it became half a century later when Martineau Street was closed. The young woman in the shortish skirt and the men pushing their bicycles across Corporation Street are coming from the row of impressive shops that were built in the 1880s between Cherry Street and Bull Street. These were known as Cobden Chambers and included the Cobden Hotel at the Cherry Street end and, halfway along, the North Western Arcade, with Winchester Chambers beyond towards Bull Street. On the corner next to the open-top tram is Corporation Street's junction with Bull Street, where the original Lewis's store has its canvas sunblinds pulled down. The lack of any other vehicles is most noticeable, with only one car to be seen. After the Great War this situation would change dramatically.

By about 1949, the date of the second photograph, the character of Corporation Street has only slightly changed. The main alteration is the new Lewis's store of 1929, built between Bull Street and Old Square. The Cobden Hotel and the associated Cobden Chambers are occupied at street level by a number of shops, including, just to the left of the bus, Spencer's jewellery shop. On the corner of Cherry Street is a large Dolcis shoe shop. The children's department in the basement had two fascinating features. On the way downstairs there was the largest aquarium ever seen by any child anywhere in Birmingham – or so it seemed! There was also a machine that by today's standards would be regarded as lethal: for the price of a penny one could X-ray one's own feet, which no one would contemplate 50 years later without a lead shield and an expert radiologist! The largest shop in this block belongs to costume-maker Austin Walter, occupying the five odd-numbered units from 71 to 79.

One of the 1914 UEC-built bogie tramcars, 537, is pulling out of Martineau Street, working on the 3X service to Witton via Aston Cross. In front of it is a pre-war Birmingham Corporation Daimler COG5 double-decker, which is going to Kingstanding on the peak-hour-only 25 service. Beyond the tram are two outward-bound open-balconied four-wheeled trams. The cars following the tram are a couple of Morrises, the front one being a Twelve Series III of 1938. By way of contrast, a horse and cart is emerging from Martineau Street. Horses were only phased out on short city journeys after local bakers and milkmen turned to battery-operated vehicles in a large way in the 1950s, and when British Railways finally turned to mechanical rather than horse-power at the end of that decade.

Only the distant tower of the Central Methodist Hall and the former Lewis's store have survived the upheavals of the 1960s in this central part of Corporation Street. On the left in August 1999 is Rackham's, which by this time was the last department store in the city centre. Opened in November 1960, it has outlived The Beehive in Albert Street (closed 29 February 1972), Edward Grey's in Bull Street (February 1973), the Birmingham Co-operative Society in High Street (1 February 1985) and Lewis's (13 July 1991). Rackham & Matthews first opened a store in Bull Street in 1881 and gradually expanded to premises in Temple Street and the North Western Arcade. It was never a real 'threat' to the other department stores in the city centre until 1955 when it was taken over by Harrods. This financial investment resulted in the construction of a new Corporation Street store, which occupied the site through to Temple Street on the Cherry Street side and the Corporation Street frontage as far as North Western Arcade. The canopy on the right belongs to the buildings constructed as part of the Commercial Union scheme that replaced Martineau Street. If, architecturally, the Rackham's building has some merit, the whole of the Commercial Union development can only be described as early 1960s utilitarian and uninspired. The 'semi-pedestrianisation' of Corporation Street has resulted in the pavements being widened and a few trees being planted, but compared with the New Street end and the northern section beyond James Watt Street and Newton Street by the Victoria Law Courts, this section has really lost its character and soul, though in all honesty it does look worse on this rainy summer's day. *Commercial postcard/Lacey's Studios/DRH*

Throughout this book photographs of trams, trolleybuses and buses figure prominently, being an integral part of central Birmingham's street scenes, but the temptation to show views dominated by these modes of transport has to be tempered by the need to show what the city looked like in years gone by. Although this is basically a 'tram' photograph, it captures what **ALBERT STREET** looked like in 1949, when it was dominated by the Beehive Store. Owned by Charles Richards, it was throughout its history of more than a century of service always regarded as a family-run enterprise. It was known as 'a warehouse for the people' and internally was far more basic than Grey's or the Co-op, selling everything from household goods to coats and suits. For many years it had an overhead money and bill-paying cable system whereby small brass canisters were sent to a central point in the store for all the bills and change to be processed.

Tram 403, one of the first UEC-built four-wheelers of the 401 class that entered service in the summer of 1912 and which soon afterwards were introduced on the Moseley Road routes, stands outside the impressive shelters on the east side of Albert Street. The shelters covered the pavement and stood against Foster Brothers gentlemen's outfitters and the Beehive store. The tram is working the 42 service to Alcester Lanes End via Digbeth, Bradford Street and Moseley Village, and this will be the last year that the Moseley Road services are worked by tramcars, as they will be replaced on 1 October. Historically this was an important event, as it was the last tram route in Britain to operate open-balconied, four-wheeled trams on a 3ft 6in gauge system. Above the tram are the double overhead wires for the Coventry Road trolleybuses that will continue to use Albert Street until they too are abandoned on 30 June 1951. Behind the tram is the bottom end of Martineau Street

at the High Street/Dale End junction (see pages 91-95), while to the left is the entrance to New Meeting Street (see pages 38-41).

Albert Street itself was named after Queen Victoria's beloved Consort and opened in 1862 as a link between the town's original railway station in Curzon Street and High Street. Unfortunately, the Borough Council was rather slow in approving the line of the road, and by the time it was completed Prince Albert had succumbed the previous year to typhoid fever and Curzon Street had been replaced as a major railway station by the opening of New Street Station. Within a few years, instead of the carriages that had originally been envisaged, horse-drawn freight wagons were using Albert Street to carry goods into the town from Curzon Street, which had become an important goods station. Always something of a road leading to nowhere, it seemed to be dependent upon the Beehive Store and its later importance as a tram, trolleybus and bus terminus. The intention to add another commercial street into the town centre was somewhat curtailed, as below its junction with Moor Street were Fazeley Street, Park Street with its gardens, and Bartholomew Street, with its church and graveyard. In

the last years of the 19th century the bottom of Albert Street was used as the CBT horse-tram terminus for the Nechells route, while in later years it became the loading-up point for the Corporation's electric tram services to Acocks Green, Bordesley Green, Hall Green and Yardley. Between January 1934 and June 1951 the street also became the terminus for the Coventry Road trolleybus services.

The present-day Albert Street is a shadow of its former self. In the 1990s its original exit into High Street was built over by the red multi-gabled building and the road was diverted into Dale End, where the Travel West Midlands Wright-bodied Volvo B10L is lying over. The new building had originally been the site of Taylor's Bank, set up in 1765 and forming the basis of Lloyds Bank, but now contains a large MacDonald's, an Allsports sportswear shop and a number of leisure-wear clothes shops. On the original line of Albert Street a few of the mid-Victorian buildings remain, one of them occupied by the Rajdoot, one of the city centre's premier Indian restaurants. All the buildings on the right of Albert Street, including the Royal Air Force recruitment 'depot' on the corner with Dale End, Foster Brothers, Baylis's wholesalers and the lamented Beehive Warehouse have long since been demolished. Perversely this has led to Albert Street resuming its original primary function as an important transport link, giving access to Dale End for buses from Chelmsley Wood and Stechford.
F. Lloyd Jones/DRH

Joseph Chamberlain's grand designs for **CORPORATION STREET** were first proposed in his 'Improvement Scheme' of 1874. The 66-feet-wide Corporation Street cut a swathe through the Georgian properties between New Street and Old Square, and by the early 1880s the 'Parisian Boulevard' had reached the junction with **BULL STREET**. Unfortunately, the initial commercial success of the scheme was already being overtaken by the economic stagnation and political climate of the 1880s, and this is evident from this circa 1891 photograph, when the elaborate Winchester Chambers Building on the left in Corporation Street is compared with the less impressive building on the corner with Bull Street, while the twin-Flemish-gabled building in Bull Street occupied by Curtis & Curtis is even more restrained. This last building marked the temporary ending of the Corporation Street development, as next door, on the extreme right, is one of the surviving Georgian premises in Bull Street, which would surprisingly survive into the early years of the 20th century. The premises are being let by Thomas Pinson of 45 Temple Street, an estate agent that still trades today in premises in Edgbaston. Winchester

Chambers was built in 1884 and included in its frontage the entrance to the North Western Arcade. This was a continuation of the original Great Western Arcade, which ran from Colmore Row, opposite the entrance to Snow Hill Station, to Temple Row. The later North Western Arcade, designed by W. Jenkins, continued this line and curved down quite a steep slope before emerging in Corporation Street. This stylish arcade opened on 5 April 1884 and originally contained 26 shops; the retail premises along Corporation Street were immediately occupied by Wilkinson & Riddell. The arcade was built over the Great Western Railway's tunnel that ran under the town and into Snow Hill Station. Originally the railway line was in a cutting, but in 1874 it was made into a 596-yard-long tunnel.

The rebuilding of Corporation Street began in the 1950s when the original 75-year leases of the Victorian premises expired. Yet again, the lessons of the past were not learned as the buildings on the prestigious corner site of Corporation Street and Bull Street were architecturally most disappointing, as can be seen in the 1999 photograph. Such a prominent position deserved better than this, but it must be remembered that the previous

Victorian premises were little better! On the skyline to the left is Rackham's department store, which dominates Corporation Street between Cherry Street and the North Western Arcade; designed by T. P. Bennett & Sons in 1957, it was completed in November 1960. The large building in Bull Street on the right is Windsor House, which occupies the Bull Street-Temple Street section of this large development. Unfortunately, the corner of Corporation Street and Bull Street has a rather uninspired four-storey block of shops and offices whose frontage has always been restricted by its proximity to a pedestrian underpass. As with other underpasses already mentioned, this one has been removed, and once again the corner of Corporation Street and Bull Street is at street level. This is an added advantage if and when the Midland Metro tram route is extended into the city centre by way of Bull Street from its present terminus in Snow Hill Station. In the foreground is a Gallic-styled column, which looks more like a *pissoir* than an advertising hoarding! *J. Whybrow collection/DRH*

The section of **BULL STREET** between Corporation Street and the top of Snow Hill was a much wider thoroughfare than the older High Street end (see page 91). In the first photograph, taken in about 1913, very few of the old Georgian and Regency buildings have been replaced, although Edward Grey has occupied most of the buildings on the left between Temple Street and the junction with Colmore Row. Grey's opened its Bull Street premises in 1891, and for more than 80 years played a major role in the history of the street. It advertised itself as 'Birmingham's Own Store', and was for many years regarded as a little more refined then some of the other city centre departmental stores. Beyond the row of Grey's shops can just be made out the tall hotel frontage of Snow Hill Station on the corner of Snow Hill and Colmore Row, and the station beyond. Just to the right, about to descend Snow Hill, is a top-covered

Corporation electric tramcar; these replaced the CBT cable-cars on the Hockley and New Inns service after the company lease expired on Friday 30 June 1911. This distant tramcar and the motor-van travelling towards Corporation Street are the only motorised vehicles in sight; if they had known the expression in the early years of King George V's reign, the shoppers have converted Bull Street into a 'pedestrianised' street and their progress is interrupted only by a young lad pedalling a tricycle cart.

The bomb-damaged corner of Temple Street at its junction with Bull Street, seen in the second photograph dated September 1954, reflects the enormous damage that occurred in the city centre during the Second World War. Dominating Bull Street is Edward Grey's department store of 1926, built when this upper section of Bull Street was widened to 80 feet. The store had a lucky escape in late October 1940 when a bomb exploded in front of it, killing several people and leaving a large crater. To the left of Grey's, occupying a 19th-century building, is one of the numerous J. Lyons restaurants that were so common throughout the city centre in the early post-war years. Next to it is a Maypole grocery and provisions shop, something that today would not even be contemplated as a commercial outlet in the city centre, while next to it is Meeson's confectionery shop. Naylor's shoe repairers are occupying the remains of a distinctly war-ravaged building. The distant bus is a 1950-built Crossley DD42/7, working on the 15B service to Garretts Green. The illuminated bollards of the newly introduced zebra crossing read 'PASS EITHER SIDE', showing that in 1954 Bull Street was still a one-way street, although this would change periodically over the succeeding years as part of the ever-altering city traffic management schemes.

The strangely lifeless view of Bull Street on 8 February 1972 shows the original Edward Grey department store about to enter its last year of independent retailing, being taken over by the Debenhams Group at the end of February 1973 and finally closing at the end of the 1980s. The late-1950s block occupied by Stead & Simpson's shoe shop is contemporary with the Rackham's block on the corner of Bull Street and Temple Street, and occupies the bomb-site in the previous photograph. Outside is parked a 1970-built Leyland FG K.30 delivery van, with its 'threepenny-bit' cab. The van, owned by Lyons Cakes, is making a delivery to what had been the Lyon's restaurant, but which has been 'trendily'

renamed 'Jolyon'. Unfortunately, the revamped image rather failed to save the former 'Nippy restaurants', all of which had disappeared by the end of the decade. The young woman with the smock-top over her flared trousers crossing the road on the left is carrying a Werff carrier bag, having just made her purchases in the shop next door to the Jolyon restaurant. On the right is the classically styled Lewis's store and The Minories, a strange passageway open to the sky but with a multi-storey bridge at first-floor level linking the two halves of Lewis's. The Minories had a rubber-bricked roadway running through it, although it was only ever used by pedestrians, except for a period at the start of the 1960s when bus services were diverted during the reconstruction of part of Corporation Street. In the background the former Great Western Hotel, concourse and booking hall were all demolished by the beginning of 1970, leaving the canopies over the station platforms visible from Bull Street, though these would themselves be pulled down during 1976.

Bull Street by 1999 had become a 'Buses Only' street with mature trees gracing a central loading island for the buses using the street as a city terminus. Travel West Midlands bus 2720 (A720 UOE), an MCW 'Metrobus' Mk II, has arrived early in Bull Street working on the M79 service to Wolverhampton, and is waiting to move down to the loading-up stop outside the Colmore Gate commercial development. Only the old Werff premises on the corner of Temple Street and those next door survive from 1972. The corner building is now called Aspect Court and has on 12 November 1999 some 22,255 sq ft of refurbished office space to let. On the ground floor is

Blacks, the ladies' fashion shop and a successor soul-mate to Werff. Dominating Bull Street is the tower of Colmore Gate, opened in 1997. This blue-and-grey-glass-clad tower extends at a lower level into Bull Street and has the same frontage that was formerly occupied by the 1926 Edward Grey store. There is no departmental store here today, as the units are mainly fast-food outlets catering for hungry, baguette-eating office workers, although there is a wine bar, and HMSO has its prestigious premises here. On the right the refurbished former Lewis's store has been cleaned, but what looked large 50 years ago now looks tiny when compared to Colmore Gate.

In the early 1970s, lack of economic investment made parts of central Birmingham look decidedly run-down, and this was true of Bull Street. The days of the big department stores were rapidly coming to a close, and while Lewis's valiantly refurbished its shop in a vain attempt to capture customers, Grey's had been in terminal decline for a while. Not even the Debenham's take-over could revive its fortunes and it was a relief to see the old store pulled down in 1994 rather than endure a succession of partial occupations by cheap Yuletide cut-price operators! One of its last uses was for auctions of cheap imported radios and hi-fi equipment, and it was rather like watching a stately old transatlantic passenger liner being used for day trips around the bay. Today, partly pedestrianised, Bull Street looks much better, although the sheer size of Colmore Gate tends to cast deep shadows over much of it for large parts of the day. At the time of writing, access to Colmore Row was blocked or restricted by the filling-in of Colmore Circus *Commercial postcard/Birmingham City Engineer & Surveyor's Dept/ Birmingham Public Works Department/DRH*

On 28 February 1957 Edward Grey's Bull Street store is flying the Union flag high above the temporary shops on either side of the entrance to the Gret Western Arcade in **COLMORE ROW**. Viewed from Livery Street alongside Snow Hill Station, the lady selling flowers from the wicker baskets doesn't seem to be doing very good business. Parked in front of her is a Ford Zodiac 206E, registered in Birmingham in 1956, while speeding up Colmore Row is a Standard Vanguard Phase I saloon. The buildings occupied by the Kardomah Coffee House and the single-storey extension to Boots the Chemist show just how much Birmingham's city centre was patched up after the war – there were similar 'temporary' shop premises in the Bull Ring, High Street and Martineau Street. Those seen here were to survive until the end of the 1950s, while the Dutch-gabled Boots shop on the Bull Street corner was pulled down during the first phase of the development of Colmore Circus and replaced by a steep staircased entrance to a pedestrian subway, still with us today. The need for redevelopment was undoubtedly necessary, but it is quite awful that attractive city centre retail premises were unnecessarily pulled down. The bus shelters on the left, which lasted until the mid-1960s, were built when the Dudley and Wednesbury trams were still running before the war, and the cobbled road surface coming out of Livery Street clearly marks the line of the old tram tracks, last used 18 years earlier on 2 April 1939. The bus shelter on the right is one of an impressive line that continued all the way alongside the Cathedral churchyard. The first is for the 3A service to Harborne and Ridgacre Road, while after 11.00pm the night service bus to Quinton, the NS9, used this stop every hour, on the hour.

Only the corner of Livery Street and the Prudential Assurance Building on the right remain on 19 May 1999. The corner of Colmore Row and Bull Street now accommodates the huge Colmore Gate complex, while next door is an attractive seven-storey row of offices and shops. The Ford Mondeo is passing the entrance to the Great Western Arcade, whose sign, just visible through the trees, is arched over the colonnade's entrance in the style of a steam locomotive nameplate. The planting of trees in this part of Colmore Row has softened the city centre environment somewhat and is a pleasant extension of the greenery in nearby St Philip's Cathedral churchyard. As was the case in 1957, it is still possible for vehicles to turn left into Colmore Row from Livery Street, a throw-back to when the electric trams on the Handsworth, West Bromwich, Wednesbury and Dudley services used Snow Hill Station as a very large terminal loop. A narrow piece of central kerb is just visible in the middle of Colmore Row, separating the majority of the traffic coming from Colmore Circus, such as the Mondeo, from that using Livery Street. *Birmingham City Engineer & Surveyor's Dept/DRH*

INDEX